Raising a Child with Autism

of related interest

Parents' Education as Autism Therapists
Applied Behaviour Analysis in Context
Edited by Mickey Keenan, Ken P. Kerr and Karola Dillenberger
ISBN 978 1 85302 778 9

Learning to Live with High Functioning Autism
A Parent's Guide for Professionals
Mike Stanton
ISBN 978 1 85302 915 8

I am Special
Introducing Children and Young People to
the Autistic Spectrum Disorder
Peter Vermeulen
ISBN 978 1 85302 916 5

Asperger's Syndrome
A Guide for Parents and Professionals
Tony Attwood
ISBN 978 1 85302 577 8

Enabling Communication in Children with Autism
Carol Potter and Chris Whittaker
ISBN 978 1 85302 956 1

**Our Journey Through High Functioning Autism
and Asperger Syndrome**
A Roadmap
Edited by Linda Andron
ISBN 978 1 85302 947 9

A Positive Approach to Autism
Stella Waterhouse
ISBN 978 1 85302 808 3

Growing Up Severely Autistic
They Call Me Gabriel
Kate Rankin
ISBN 978 1 85302 891 5

Breaking Autism's Barriers
A Father's Story
Bill Davis, as told to Wendy Goldband Schunick
ISBN 978 1 85302 979 0

Raising a Child with Autism

A Guide To Applied Behavior Analysis For Parents

Shira Richman

Jessica Kingsley Publishers
London and Philadelphia

First published in the United Kingdom in 2001
by Jessica Kingsley Publishers
116 Pentonville Road
London N1 9JB, UK
and
400 Market Street, Suite 400
Philadelphia, PA 19106, USA

www.jkp.com

Library of Congress Cataloging in Publication Data
Richman, Shira. 1972-
   Raising a child with autism: a guide to applied behavior for parents / Shira Richman.
      p. cm.
   Includes bibliographical references.
   ISBN 1-85302-910-6 (alk. paper)
   1. Autistic children. 2. Autistic children--Behavior modification. 3. Parents of autistic
children. 4. Autism. I. Title

RJ506.A9 R535 2000
618.92'8982--dc21

00-047818

British Library Cataloguing in Publication Data
A CIP catalogue record for this book is available from the British Library

ISBN 978 1 85302 910 3

Printed and bound in the United States by
Thomson-Shore, Inc.

Contents

In loving memory of Leon Lantz, my grandfather and my inspiration as a writer and as an individual.

To Evan, my husband, for always believing in me and for his unconditional love and support, without which I could not have written this book.

With special thanks to our parents, Esther and Mervin Verbit and Miriam and Paul Richman, for raising us with much patience and love.

Thank you to all the children with whom I have worked, to their wonderful parents, and to the professionals who taught me much along the way.

CHAPTER I

What is Autism?

Signs and symptoms of autism

Autism is a pervasive developmental disorder that affects approximately ten to fifteen out of every ten thousand children. Its onset usually occurs prior to thirty months of age, but only becomes easily detectable when the child's failure to develop communicative language becomes apparent.

Childhood disintegrative disorder shares the same symptoms as autism, but in this condition normal development is exhibited for the first two years of life, followed by a significant loss of previously acquired skill. Autism occurs in boys about three times as often as it occurs in girls, and its specific etiology is not yet known.

The diagnostic standard used to identify autism is called the *Diagnostic and Statistical Manual of Mental Disorders* of the American Psychiatric Association, fourth edition, or the DSM-IV, published in 1994. It includes twelve diagnostic criteria grouped into three categories: social interaction, communication, and activities and interests. Individuals affected with autism will not necessarily have all of the signs and symptoms associated with the disorder. Although they may exhibit similar symptoms, no two children with autism are alike. In order to be diagnosed with autism, a child must exhibit two criteria from the first category, two criteria from the second category, and one from the third. Here is a closer look at each diagnostic category within the DSM-IV:

Social interaction

Children with autism do not have proper use and understanding of nonverbal behaviors, nor do they exhibit age-appropriate social interaction. A child with autism may:

- exhibit little if any eye contact
- be unable to read facial expressions or respond to social cues and gestures, such as waving and pointing
- fail to interact and to develop appropriate peer relationships
- prefer isolation and appear uninterested in other people
- use people as tools by guiding their hands in order to retrieve an object that the child desires
- exhibit minimal or no initiation and play skills.

In infancy a child with autism may not exhibit an anticipatory response to being picked up and may not like to be held. He may not play peek-a-boo or visually follow the coming and going of his caregiver. As a toddler, the child may not exhibit normal stranger anxiety, and may show either little or extreme attachment to people.

Communication

Children with autism show qualitative disturbances in speech as well as quantitative ones. In other words, the speech of children with autism is not merely delayed, but is not evenly developed. Inappropriate use of language may include:

- echolalia (rote repetition of words and/or phrases)
- a monotonous tone lacking pitch or intonation
- lack of social imitative play and spontaneity and variation in language use
- pronoun reversals
- a discrepancy between receptive and expressive language with no concept of abstractions such as danger.

Approximately forty percent of children with autism do not develop language at all, nor do they try to compensate through the use of alternative methods of communication such as gestures or mime. Those who do develop speech do not use their speech skills to converse with others appropriately.

In infancy, a child with autism may be overly quiet, not crying or cooing appropriately. He may show few signs of intentional communication with gestures or with verbalizations, and may fail to imitate words or sounds.

As a toddler, the child may lose the words he had previously.

Activities and interests

Children with autism develop repetitive motor mannerisms and/or stereotyped patterns of behavior that can be manifested in a variety of ways. A child with autism may:

- exhibit stereotypies and repetitive patterns of behavior such as hand-flapping, hand-regarding, eye-gazing, body-rocking, grimacing, tapping, and vocalizations
- become abnormally focused on one pattern of behavior or routine, exhibiting a need for sameness
- have an abnormal interaction with toys that may include an extreme focus on parts of objects.

A pattern of behavior may also be restrictive with regard to one or more sense modality. Abnormal responses to sensory stimulation may have various manifestations:

- a child with autism may have an overstimulated or understimulated tactile focus
- olfactory and taste sensitivities may be an issue
- abnormal visual stimulation may include such behaviors as the lining up of toys or figures, obsessing over patterning configurations, letters and numbers, and eye-gazing in various lights

○ reactions to sound may be extreme. A child may not be able to filter out background noise. He may overreact to auditory stimulation, or may not react at all.

In infancy, this may mean that a child refuses foods of various tastes and textures. It may mean that he or she appears deaf to human voices and environmental sounds, or jumps at environmental sounds in a panic. Infants may react to certain fabrics as well. As a toddler, a child with autism may engage in self-stimulation and rather stare into space than play with toys. He may spend a lot of time spinning the wheel of a car, or lining blocks and animals on the edge of a table.

Children with autism are similar in many ways, exhibiting deficits in some areas of development and excesses in others. Nevertheless, for each child, these 'splinter skills' are different and unique. Not all of the above symptoms need be present in order for the child to be diagnosed as having autistic disorder. Each symptom, however, is a part of the autistic syndrome, and if enough are present, a child will be diagnosed.

Due to the complexity of autism and the fact that symptoms emerge over time, a behavioral and developmental history usually accompanies behavioral observation before a formal diagnosis is given. Medical tests may also be conducted in order to rule out other possible causes such as infections and allergies.

Current prognosis

Autism affects all major areas of functioning. Although diagnoses can change, the majority of children diagnosed with autistic disorder keep that diagnosis. Since autism can develop different signs and symptoms throughout a child's development, and since some therapies can be successful in teaching skills to children with autism, the severity of a child's autism may change over time.

In order to chart these changes in a child's clinical profile, a number of autism rating scales have been developed. Two popular rating scales are the *Childhood Autism Rating Scale* (CARS) and the *Autism Behavior Checklist*.

The CARS rating scale was developed by Eric Schopler and his colleagues. It is a checklist that is made to classify a child according to the severity of his autism, and can be easily updated as the child matures and his symptoms evolve. School programs often use this and similar rating scales in order to chart the learning that occurred for each child during a school year.

The *Autism Behavior Checklist* rates each behavior exhibited by the child with autism. It concludes with a comprehensive rating of the severity of the disorder as presented in the child. The *Autism Behavior Checklist* is often used in schools as well.

IQ tests may also be given to children with autism. Statistics show that they tend to score significantly higher on the performance intelligence section than on the verbal intelligence section. Most score in the 'mild to moderate mental retardation' range. It is interesting to note, however, that in the UCLA Young Autism Project conducted by Ivar Lovaas and colleagues, children who received intensive one-on-one behavioral intervention not only achieved behavioral gains but also showed an increase in their IQ scores that proved significant and was maintained over time (see p.14).

Indeed, it is difficult to assess whether or not the IQ score of a child with autism is accurate. The IQ test is designed to evaluate a child's cognitive functioning level in various areas and, by doing so, predict future performance. It does not consider motivational level, ability to generalize skills and work in new settings with new and unfamiliar materials, distraction level and ability to focus, etc. These are all factors that could affect the performance of a child with autism in an IQ test.

There are cases in which children with autism have been mainstreamed, even to the point of receiving a new diagnosis. More often, however, gains are more subtle and changes occur over time in various symptoms, some improving and others evolving as learning occurs.

The history of diagnosis and believed causation

Autism was first identified by Leo Kanner in 1943. Leo Kanner was an American child psychiatrist who saw distinctions between autism and childhood schizophrenia and labeled autism as a separate disorder. He identified autism based on two key elements which he described as 'autistic aloneness' and 'desire for sameness', along with other behavioral idiosyncrasies and varying isolated abilities.

The word 'autism' is derived from the Greek word *autos*, meaning self. Interestingly, Hans Asperger chose the same word in his second doctoral thesis, submitted that same year, 1943, to describe similar yet higher functioning children. The syndrome Asperger described is now known as Asperger's syndrome. It differs from autism in that the onset is usually later, social and communication deficits are less severe, and it includes an overwhelming preoccupation with specific areas of interest. Asperger's paper was published in German in 1944 and later translated into English in 1991.

The children first observed with autism were mostly from the middle-to-upper-class and had parents who could afford private psychiatric treatment. Much blame for the syndrome was placed on the mother. In the 1960s, Bruno Bettelheim published *The Empty Fortress*, in which he expressed his opinion that autism is caused by rejection of the child by the parent. He believed that parents of children with autism were cold toward their children. Combined with the prevalent trend toward psychoanalysis, this led him to believe that parental rejection caused a child to withdraw from the world into an autistic-like state. He coined the term 'refrigerator mother' to reflect the role he believed the mother played in her child's autism.

By the mid 1960s Ivar Lovaas had already begun his work with children with autism. He is best known, however, for the study he conducted in the early 1970s, using behavior modification and applied behavior analysis as therapy in intensive, one-on-one settings. In this study, he worked with nineteen autistic children, nine of whom he reported as having achieved 'normal functioning.' In 1973 he published his study. His positive scientific results proved very significant. Society began to believe that autism was not a result of the mother's actions and her child's subsequent defense mechanism, but rather resulted from one or more of the following:

- genetic causes

- risk factors associated with pregnancy and delivery

- an unidentifiable genetic mutation

- environmental factors.

In 1977 the Autism Society of America published the first definition of autism, and by 1980 the American Psychiatric Association included a definition of the syndrome in the *Diagnostic Statistical Manual*, which has since been revised. Autism has now been found throughout the world across races, ethnicities and social backgrounds.

The specific etiology of autism is not yet known. The predominant view, however, is still that autism has a biological origin and that the disorder's manifestations may be further affected by environmental factors. The pioneer in searching for the biological origins of autism is Bernard Rimland, himself the father of an adult with autism. Bernard Rimland also developed the oldest autism rating scale and founded The American National Society for Autistic Children.

Various treatments and educational methods

Note that the author is not recommending all of these methods, nor deeming them all effective in treating children with autism.

1. *Psychoanalysis*

Psychoanalysis was the standard method of treatment from the 1940s to the 1960s and is still used, though infrequently, for children who have been diagnosed as having autistic disorder. In the past, psychoanalysis for children with autism often began by separating the child from his or her mother and caring for the child in a residential program. There the child would be provided with love and a supportive environment, particularly during episodes of difficult behavior.

Often, autistic symptoms were analyzed and interpreted. Such subjective, emotional interpretations are a part of psychoanalysis today. Mothers are usually instructed to undergo psychoanalysis with their children, and are often blamed for their child's autism.

2. Diet

Most of the diets used to treat children with autism were originally constructed for children with attention deficit disorder and hyperactivity. The diets were adapted for the treatment of autism by some dietitians who believe that it is a lack of tolerance for certain food substances that leads a child with autism to food selectivity and idiosyncratic eating habits.

Diet treatments usually include the elimination of preservatives and other additives from the child's food intake. Some diets also eliminate the child's intake of yeast, soy, milk, wheat, sugar and/or other substances.

No studies have evaluated whether or not children with autism actually have difficulty tolerating these substances, and it is left to families to decide whether or not the special diets are having a positive effect on the child's behavior. Medications have also been adapted.

3. Facilitated communication

In facilitated communication a parent or caregiver touches the child and helps him to point to letters or words in order to promote communication. This method of intervention was originally designed for individuals with neuro-motor disorders such as cerebral palsy, and became popular in the early 1990s.

Facilitated communication claimed to lead individuals with autism to communicate their inner thoughts and feelings. All claims to its effectiveness, however, were subjective and presented by individuals with personal and emotional investments in the method. Studies conducted by the American Psychological Association in

1994 revealed that many of the communications were actually produced by the facilitators themselves, some consciously and some subconsciously.

4. Auditory training

Auditory training was developed by a physician named Guy Berard. In auditory training, an audiogram identifies frequencies to which the child with autism is hypersensitive. Once these frequencies are determined, they are eliminated from an audio-recording that the child listens to through headphones during therapy sessions.

Auditory training usually consists of ten hours of sessions spread over two weeks. Parents are often advised to discontinue all other therapies until the training is complete.

Although auditory training gained popularity in the early 1990s, there is no evidence to suggest that hypersensitive hearing causes maladaptive behaviors. Furthermore, there is no scientific evidence that listening to music can alter auditory sensitivity.

5. Sensory integration

Sensory integration is usually given by occupational therapists and has been popular for approximately twenty-five years. It is often recommended for children with autism who engage in inappropriate responses to sensory stimuli (examples of such inappropriate responses include tapping and body-rocking.) Therapy consists of the child swinging from a device that is attached to the ceiling, receiving massages, having his extremities brushed by the therapist, and other enjoyable activities, which should help to relax a child on a short-term basis.

Results of sensory integration therapy are measured subjectively and the progress of children receiving it has been shown to be no different from that of children with autism who have not participated in sensory integration. There is no evidence that these activities affect the way in which the brain processes sensory stimulations.

6. Holding therapy

Holding therapy became popular in the late 1980s. It was developed by a New York psychologist and has remnants of the belief that autism is caused by the parents. In holding therapy, the parents hold their child throughout his struggling, until a few minutes of calmness have passed. During the holding the parent is supposed to be face-to-face with the child, and it is sometimes recommended that the parent use this opportunity to shout out his or her feelings to the child.

Through many sessions of holding therapy, the child with autism is supposed to feel loved and 'emerge.' When holding is not successful, the parents are usually blamed and accused of having little dedication to the cause. Although holding may indeed provide tactile stimulation, and face-to-face holding may increase eye contact for short periods of time, it has not been shown to lead directly to increased socialization or skill acquisition.

7. Options therapy

Options therapy was designed by Barry Neil Kaufman and Samahria Lyke Kaufman for their son, Raun, who was diagnosed with severe autism at eighteen months. Their story is described in their book *Son Rise*. Options therapy consists of remaining in a confined space with the autistic child and, rather than placing demands on him or her, showing complete acceptance. This is accomplished by imitating the child's every movement.

In the book *Son Rise* there is a breakthrough, and the child is said to have emerged. However, there is no research showing the benefits of this approach, and it is not completely clear whether or not the professionals who were said to have diagnosed the boy all agreed that he was actually autistic prior to treatment. Although imitation is an important skill, mirroring a child's movements can encourage inappropriate behaviors as well as appropriate ones. The options method does not teach a child any additional skills, nor does it expand on a child's previously established repertoire.

8. Music/art/dance therapies

There is merit in teaching fine arts to children with developmental delays. Fine arts therapies have been shown to be calming, and have helped children with motor coordination difficulties, emotional issues and more. Such therapies may even be effective in reducing difficult behaviors on a short-term basis.

Although there may be benefits to having a child work with an artist, there is no evidence that engaging in these therapies increases cognition or teaches necessary skills to autistic children. To accomplish these goals, additional work would be necessary.

9. TEACCH

Eric Schopler developed the TEACCH approach in the early 1970s. TEACCH works with each student as an individual, studying the 'culture of autism' with the belief that there is no such thing as 'normal' behavior. Individuals with autism present similar characteristics, but in this approach are not believed to be inferior to the rest of society.

Teaching is conducted by cultivating a student's pre-existing strengths and interests, focusing less on deficits that need work. Structure is highly stressed, e.g. organizing the physical environment, creating work schedules and using visual materials. These techniques can be very effective but are often not sufficiently hands-on. Behavioral programs (see below: applied behavior analysis) incorporate these techniques, and others with a different backing philosophy, while tracking individual progress precisely in order to ensure both behavioral progress and acquisition of skills.

10. Applied behavior analysis

Applied behavior analysis (ABA) follows the accepted theory that autism is neurologically based and that it is a syndrome that affects a variety of behaviors. ABA deals with these behavioral excesses and deficits by manipulating the environment systematically so that wanted behaviors are taught and reinforced. Therapists who use the

ABA method teach skills in small, measurable steps, using the scientific principles that govern behavior, originally studied and proposed by B. F. Skinner. All ABA programs are individualized to fit the child's needs.

Many research studies have been conducted on the use of ABA with children with autism. These studies usually focus on a single subject, measuring the child's behavior at various points during the treatment and graphing the data to show how it is affecting the behavior.

Through repetition and practice during intensive instruction periods, autistic children can improve their behavior and increase their cognitive functioning level. Some who begin therapy at a very young age are even integrated into regular school classes.

Applied behavior analysis will be discussed at greater length in Chapter Two.

Conclusion

Autism is a pervasive developmental disorder that affects all major areas of functioning. Children diagnosed with autistic disorder exhibit symptoms from three categories:

- ◦ an impairment in their social-relatedness

- ◦ impairments in their communication skills and use of language

- ◦ repetitive and stereotyped patterns of behavior and interests.

In order to be diagnosed with autistic disorder, a child must exhibit at least two symptoms from the first category, two from the second category and one from the third.

Children with autism also exhibit uneven development and abilities, and splinter skills. Many are usually stronger at skills that require memory and object-manipulation than they are at verbal and social skills.

Though their symptoms may be similar, no two autistic children are exactly alike. Autism is a syndrome. This means that a diagnosed child will not necessarily have all of the signs and symptoms associated with the disorder. Autism rating scales are used to track the severity of a child's symptoms as they change over time.

It is currently believed that the origin of autism is biological, and that its manifestations may be further affected by environmental factors. The exact etiology of the disorder is still being researched.

Autism affects approximately ten to fifteen out of every ten thousand children. There are a variety of treatments and educational methods being implemented, but not all have been proven effective. Studies have shown that applied behavior analysis can be used to improve behavior, teach skills and increase a child's cognitive functioning level.

CHAPTER 2

Learning Theory
and Applied Behavior Analysis

Introduction: What is learning and how can behaviors be taught?

Learning can be defined as a process by which behaviors are formed. By observing these behaviors as they develop and change over time, one can easily measure learning as it takes place.

- Learning is a change in behavior.

- Learning is observable.

- Learning is measurable.

In order for one to be able to say that learning has taken place, however, the change in behavior must be maintained over time.

Applied behavior analysis is a method by which behaviors are observed and measured, and new behaviors are taught. A behavior can be understood by looking at the set of events that surround it, closely examining the events that precede and follow it. For example, to understand why a child threw a toy, it is important to examine exactly what occurred prior to that action. Perhaps the child's sister called him a name. Perhaps the child could not get the toy to work. Perhaps the toy was a ball. To understand why a child continues to throw toys, it is also important to examine what occurs after the child engages in such behavior. Perhaps throwing the toy causes the sister to leave the room. Perhaps his mother fixes the toy. Or perhaps the child wins a ball game. These consequences all tend to encourage the act of throwing.

By orchestrating the events which occur prior to and following a specific behavior, one can begin to change the behavior and, in essence, teach. Two ways to instruct through the use of learning theory and applied behavior analysis are the discrete trial method of instruction and incidental teaching.

1. Discrete trials

In a discrete trial an instructor (teacher, therapist, parent, friend, etc.) presents an Sd (discriminative stimulus)/ an instruction, and waits for the child to respond. If the child responds correctly, the consequence is that the instructor reinforces the child's response by praising the child and perhaps even rewarding her for a job well done. If the child responds incorrectly, the instructor immediately prompts her, ensuring that he does respond appropriately. This prompt is carried out in order to teach the child the correct behavioral response to the instruction. **Sd (discriminative stimulus)/instruction > Sr (response stimulus) > reinforcement or prompt.**

For example, the instructor tells the child to put on her hat, and then guides her hands in order to help her do so. Learning can be said to have occurred once the child follows the instruction independently. Discrete trials are often repeated until some learning has taken place, and continued later on in order to ensure that the change in behavior, i.e. that which was learned, is maintained over time.

Discrete trials are beneficial in that they provide children with intensive instruction and direct feedback. They can be individualized to meet the child's academic needs, and progress can be tracked via trial-by-trial recording of accurate data, which is later graphed for easy reading.

2. Incidental teaching

By controlling or limiting a child's access to materials, one can cause him to initiate throughout the day. He will have to initiate in order to ask for the materials that he needs. For example, if a mother removes the crayons from the closet before asking her child to color, he will learn to ask for the crayons. The skill of asking for a missing or needed item, in this example, was taught incidentally. Other examples of incidental teaching include asking a child to read in a dark room so that he will initiate turning on the light, sitting down to dinner without forks on the table (though here the child may begin to solve the problem by eating with his hands), and holding a child's favorite toy to get him to request it. It is important, when staging these situations, to prompt him to respond correctly if, at first, he is unable to do so. Although prompts are used in discrete trials, by incorporating prompts into incidental teaching and repeating each example a number of times, learning can be facilitated.

This overview of the behavioral approach is by no means comprehensive. Other teaching strategies that are applied in school, after school, and in home-based programs for children with autism include, but are not limited to, the following:

- teaching for generalization
- shaping
- chaining.

All of the techniques mentioned above and their application to a home setting will be addressed in this chapter. Additional terms used in the field appear and are discussed in future chapters, as well.

Sd (discriminative stimulus)

A discriminative stimulus is any instruction that is presented in order to elicit a specific response. For example:

Sd = 'Please go get your coat.'

In order for an Sd, or an instruction, to be effective, it must be understood. Children, especially those with autism, need instructions to be presented in a clear, directive voice. The instruction should be brief and specific, with a clear onset and offset. Rambling instructions are more difficult to follow. To illustrate, 'Could you please go find your coat, I think that it may be in the closet, but I am not sure,' is a much more difficult Sd than 'Please go to the closet and get your coat.' Speaking to a child in clear and easily understood sentences will help her comprehension and direction-following skills.

There are a number of different types of Sds:

- verbal, as illustrated above

- visual, such as written words and pictures that symbolize instructions, or even an item in the environment, such as a puzzle, that one sees and then approaches to play

- gestural, i.e. pointing to indicate that someone should look in a certain direction or retrieve a certain object, and facial expressions.

In the home

If one thinks carefully about the Sds, or instructions, that one naturally presents during the course of the day, one can begin to work to make them more effective. If a verbal instruction is not effective in getting a child to retrieve his coat from the closet, perhaps handing him a picture of a coat along with the verbal instruction will help him to remember, once he gets to the closet, what he is expected to retrieve. (This picture can also be considered a prompt.)

Gaining a child's attention prior to presenting an instruction will ensure that she has heard the instruction. A child who is not attending will be unable to comply.

Keeping the type of Sd used for various tasks consistent across family members will benefit the child until he understands the instructions and is able to follow them consistently. Only after the child is fully competent with regard to an instruction should one consider varying the words used ('Go get the coat,' 'Please go get your coat,' 'Can you please bring me your coat.'). Once the words 'go' 'get' and 'coat' have meaning, a more elaborate sentence using these words can be comprehensible, as when one is learning a new language.

One of the most important things to remember about Sds is that one should never present an instruction unless one is prepared to follow through with it and teach the child the correct response immediately if she does not comply. This consistency will ensure that the instruction remains meaningful to the child. It will also ensure that the parent does not get into the habit of raising his or her voice. Changing the Sd in any way as a result of the child's response teaches her to listen only when the parent is angry.

For example: Kim is playing in the kitchen with the pots and pans. Mother calls down from the bedroom 'Stop playing with the pots, Kim.' Mother, however, is on the telephone, and does not follow through when Kim continues to play. Kim bangs on the pots loudly. 'Kim, I said stop making noise and put the pots away.' Kim does not comply, and mother remains on the phone. Kim bangs even louder. This time, the banging is so loud that it disturbs mother's telephone conversation. Mother yells, 'Kim, I told you to stop – I'm coming downstairs and if the pots and pans are not put away there will be no television for a week!'

In this example the mother, though not intentionally, taught Kim that she only needs to listen to her mother when mother is angry. The simple instruction, 'Stop playing with the pots, Kim,' has now lost its meaning as an Sd, because Kim was not made to respond to that instruction appropriately. Now Kim has learned that her mother is only serious when she yells. Following through with one's Sds/instructions the first time they are presented ensures that they will be effective instructions and requests in the future.

Reinforcement

Positive reinforcement is anything that, when presented immediately following a behavior, causes that behavior to increase in frequency. If a child who cleans up his toys is rewarded with the opportunity to watch cartoons, the child will probably clean up his toys again in the future.

Types of *positive* reinforcement include:

- edibles, such as cookies, chocolate, soda

- verbal, for example: 'Nice job!' 'You are the best!' 'Excellent waiting!'

○ tangible, such as a doll or a toy car

○ social, such as tickles, a pat on the back, high fives, and songs.

Negative reinforcement is the removal of an unpleasant stimulus immediately following a behavior, and causes that behavior to increase in frequency. Responding 'No' to the question 'Do you want the pickle?' is a behavior that is followed by removing the pickle from the child's plate. Removing the unpleasant smell of pickle, for a child who does not like pickles, increases the likelihood that he will use the word 'no' appropriately in the future.

Another example: An alarm buzzer in the morning (a very aversive sound) increases the likelihood that one will get out of bed because the behavior of getting out of bed is reinforced by the shutting of the alarm.

In the home

It is important to remember that what may seem reinforcing to a parent may not be reinforcing to the child. Different children also enjoy different things. If a child does not like chocolate, then, for that child, chocolate is not going to be a reinforcer. Furthermore, reinforcers need to be rotated in order to ensure that they remain effective. No one could eat cookies and only cookies forever. Having a variety of reinforcers available ensures that a child is not satiated by any specific one, and also allows the child to select an item of his choice.

When reinforcing a child's behavior, one must present the reinforcement immediately following that behavior. This way, the child is able to connect the reinforcer with the behavior, and not with a different behavior that has since occurred. Take a child who is learning to respond correctly to the Sd 'Stand up,' and happens to have a cold. The instructor says 'Stand up.' The child does, and rubs his nose. The instructor reinforces the child with a candy. The following week, after the child has recuperated, he is asked to stand up. It is very likely that in addition to standing as a response, he will still rub his nose even though his cold is now gone. Reinforcing his correct response or proper behavior immediately ensures that this is the behavior that will increase in the future.

The same rule applies for reinforcing inappropriate behavior along with the appropriate response. For example, if a child is setting the table while engaging in verbalizations that are self stimulatory, reinforcement will cause both behaviors to increase. In order to avoid this situation, prompt the child to do the task again without the verbalizations (or any other inappropriate behavior that arose) and only then reinforce.

Differential reinforcement is when the most powerful reinforcer is saved for the most difficult task. If a child loves Barney, save the Barney doll as a treat, say, for after toilet-training. Activities during the day can also be arranged in a reverse order of preference so that each activity reinforces the activity it follows. For example, if a child needs to complete a puzzle, color, and build with blocks during a play session, and hates completing puzzles but loves coloring, schedule the activities as follows: block-building, puzzle, coloring. The ability to color following the completion of a puzzle will act as a natural reinforcer.

Finally, try to fade reinforcers to more natural ones as quickly as possible. Access to a toy or activity is more natural than an edible. For verbal praise to gain reinforcing qualities, pair the praise with an edible and slowly fade away the edible. Remember that the tone of one's voice can be even more reinforcing than the actual words spoken. It is known that to an American, a Frenchman will usually sound seductive and an Englishman will sound proper. A boss can tell an employee that a job was well done and still sound disapproving. A child can interpret the words 'You did well on the test' as a consolation, when the parent actually meant them as a compliment. Praise a child with an upbeat voice in order to ensure that she knows that the words spoken to her are words of praise and encouragement.

Prompting

A prompt is any assistance that is provided along with an instruction in order to elicit/ensure a desired response or behavior. Although one wants to be as unintrusive as possible in one's prompting (in order to increase independence), it is crucial that the prompt is effective in teaching the child what he is supposed to do.

The types of prompts used by teachers and therapists are relatively easy to implement and can be used in the home to teach and promote appropriate behavioral responses.

Verbal prompts

A verbal prompt is very difficult to fade. Children with autism often tend to become dependent on verbal prompts, relying on them to indicate what the next step of an activity is. Preschoolers, for example, will often comply with the instruction 'Do the puzzle,' but then wait for it to be repeated before each puzzle piece is placed on the board. For this reason, it is best to use verbal prompts only in order to elicit verbal responses. For example, when asking a child what he wants, it is appropriate to verbally prompt a response by saying 'Say, I want to play,' and then slowly fading that prompt to 'Say, I want…' etc.

Physical prompts

A physical prompt guides a child to perform a task through physical contact. This can mean a full hand-over-hand prompt to teach a child to put a block in a bucket, or a slight tap on the shoulder to remind a her to reach for her fork.

Although they may seem to be more intrusive, physical prompts are the easiest prompts to fade. They should be used for any task that a child is being taught to complete independently, such as dressing, toilet-training, setting the table, puzzles, shape sorters and the like. In order to prompt a child to complete a shape sorter, for example, place your hand over his and physically guide him to place each shape in the sorter as it should be done. Fade this prompt as follows:

1.   As you feel the child gaining control, relax your grip. Slowly, allow him to gain independence and prompt him hand-over-hand only when he is not successful.

2. After a while, he will only need you to hold and guide his wrist toward the materials.

3. Eventually, his independence will be such that he will only need a periodic, slight tap on the shoulder as a reminder to continue the task.

4. Finally, the prompts can be faded altogether, and the child should be able to play with the shape sorter without any help.

Visual prompts

A visual prompt is similar to a visual Sd. It is a written or pictorial symbol indicating an instruction. For example: a picture of a sweater can be given to a child when she is asked to retrieve her sweater from the closet. Now she is less likely to forget the request mid-journey. This can be done for any item the child is to retrieve. A visual prompt, unlike a visual Sd, is not meant to be the main instruction. Rather, it is a tool meant to help a child learn to respond correctly to an instruction; a tool that should be faded as the child begins to respond correctly.

Positional prompts

A positional prompt is a type of visual prompt. The position of an item serves as the visual clue. For example, a full garbage bag placed at the door can be a positional prompt to remind a child of his chores. He sees the bag, and remembers to check all the cans in the house and take out the garbage before he leaves. Positional prompts are often used to help teach children matching skills. The item that matches the item that the child is holding is placed on the table among other items. It is positioned, however, closest to the child, hinting to the child that it is the proper match.

Modeling/gestures

Modeling is actually doing exactly what the child is expected to do, step by step, while the child observes so as to learn by imitation. Gestures, on the other hand, include pointing and facial expressions. They are more difficult to fade, and are sometimes even unintentional.

The most common unintentional gesture is when you open your mouth and form your lips in anticipation of a child's verbal request. You, as parents, may know that your child wants a drink after school or a specific toy and, without realizing, prompt him to say the words 'I want juice,' or 'I want Pooh.' He will now not be able to request these items without the visual prompt of your open mouth, and will never request these items of anyone other than you. The only way to avoid this situation is to be careful not to use gestural prompts that were not intended and that do not occur naturally in the environment. Useful gestural prompts include waving (see Chapter Six on communication), a 'come here' gesture of the hand, and placing a finger at one's mouth to indicate for quiet.

Note that in order for a prompt to be successful, it must be presented immediately following the Sd (see the example regarding following through with Sds, in which Kim was banging on pots in the kitchen). A child who is prompted correctly is guaranteed success at the task at hand. This success, especially when the activity is a difficult one, can decrease the anxiety associated with it and increase opportunities for verbal praise and reward. When one feels successful one is quicker to learn and happier doing so.

Prompted responses should always receive less potent reinforcement than independent responses, and prompts should be faded as quickly as possible in order to increase independence.

Generalization

Generalization occurs when a behavior demonstrated in one specific situation is exhibited in other similar situations as well. For example, Johnny is taught to say 'Thank you' when his mother gives him a cookie. This behavior is generalized once Johnny says 'Thank you' when grandpa gives him a toy, his sister shares her snack, etc.

Generalization can also mean that a response has taken on new, spontaneous variations. For example: Johnny sometimes says 'Thank you,' sometimes 'Thanks,' and sometimes 'That's great, thank you so much.'

A behavior becomes functional only once it has become generalized. If a child eats with only one specific spoon, it cannot be said that the child eats properly with utensils. For this reason, generalization is one of the most important aspects of learning.

In the home

If skills that are taught in school are practiced in the home, generalization will occur more quickly. Even skills originally taught in the home need to be generalized.

Types of generalization include:

- generalization across people, i.e. the child can respond to mother, teacher, stranger, and anyone whom he comes across
- generalization across settings, i.e. the child can respond at home, in school, in the park, at the store and throughout the community
- generalization across a variety of Sds, i.e. the child can respond to both 'Where do you live?' and 'What is your address?'
- generalization of response, i.e. the child can respond to the above question by saying '123 Smith Drive' and 'in Queens'
- generalization across time, meaning that the child remembers and exhibits the skill from day to day throughout life. This is also termed 'maintenance.'

Generalization does not always occur naturally. In order to promote generalization, it is necessary to work on skills throughout different rooms in the home and places in the community, and with a variety of people. Reinforce the skills across environments and people as naturally as possible. A child will not be able to receive a candy each time he throws a ball for the rest of his childhood, but he may naturally receive pats on the back and verbal reinforcement such as 'great throw' and 'nice teamwork.' Natural reinforcers promote generalization and help to maintain behaviors and skills over time.

Shaping

Shaping is a technique used to teach a behavior that is not in a child's repertoire and that, when taken as a whole, is too difficult for the child to be successful. When a behavior is shaped, it is taught by reinforcing successive approximations to the desired behavior. Each approximation, once learned and mastered, is expanded upon until the entire behavior is mastered. An example of shaping is as follows:

Step 1.   Kara is reinforced for saying the sound 'mm.'

Step 2.   Kara is reinforced for saying the sound 'mma.'

Step 3.   Kara is reinforced for saying the sound 'mmam.'

Step 4.   Kara is reinforced for saying 'mommy.'

It would have been unfair to expect Kara to say 'mommy' right from the start. The verbalization would have been beyond her capacity and verbal skills, and, if it was demanded of her, it would have been both impossible for her to repeat and frustrating for her and her mother. Teaching Kara successive approximations of the word and shaping her behavior slowly allows her to be successful, gain reinforcement, and learn at her own pace. (Note that her mother is a natural and appropriate reinforcer for this verbalization, once edibles are faded.)

Chaining

Chaining is very similar to shaping. Chaining refers to teaching a behavior by breaking it down into its component skills and teaching them one at a time. This way, the child learns by building on behaviors already in his repertoire. This sequencing can be done in two ways:

Forward chaining

Forward chaining is when the steps progress forward towards a complete behavior. Here is an example of how one would teach a child to make a sandwich using forward chaining. Notice that the child will learn the component skills in the order in which they are naturally completed:

1. Place a slice of bread on a plate.

2. Place a slice of turkey on the bread.

3. Spread mustard on the turkey.

4. Place a piece of lettuce on top of the mustard.

5. Place a piece of tomato on top of the lettuce.

6. Place another slice of bread on top of the tomato to complete the sandwich, and eat it.

First the child is taught Step 1. Once she masters Step 1, she is taught Steps 1 and 2. When these steps are mastered together as a chain, she is taught Steps 1, 2, 3, and so forth, until she knows how to make the sandwich in its entirety. Many complicated behaviors can be taught in the home using forward chaining – behaviors such as setting the table, going to the bathroom, washing in the shower, and more.

Backward chaining

Backward chaining is when the behavior is taught beginning with the last step and progressing backward, towards the first. It gives the child the opportunity to be rewarded more quickly, which also acts as a reinforcer. Here is the same example of making the sandwich, this time using backward chaining. Notice that the child will learn the component skills in the reverse order, as follows:

1. Place a slice of bread on top of the tomato (the rest of the sandwich must be already prepared) to complete the sandwich, and eat it.

2. Place a piece of tomato on top of the lettuce, (the beginning of the sandwich must already be prepared) and another slice of bread on top of the tomato in order to complete the sandwich, and eat it.

3. Place a piece of lettuce on top of the mustard, and continue to complete step 2, then 1.

4. Spread the mustard on the already prepared turkey and continue with steps 3, 2, 1.

5. Place a slice of turkey on an already prepared slice of bread and continue to complete the sandwich, and eat it.

6. Independently make the sandwich from beginning to end.

Although backward chaining appears to be more complicated than forward chaining, it is usually easier to teach. In a backward chaining procedure a child is only expected, at first, to complete the last step of a sequence. Once the last step is completed, the end result becomes clear and the task, or step, that was required of the child becomes functional. In this case, a child who first learns to place a slice of bread on top of an already prepared sandwich gets to see that he has now made a sandwich. Even the reinforcer is a natural one – the child can now eat the sandwich.

When chaining a behavior, prompt each new step physically from behind, as necessary, in order to increase independence (remember that verbal and gestural prompts are harder to fade).

Conclusion

Learning theory and applied behavior analysis, when studied in depth, can become very complicated and involved. By learning some of the terms in the field and applying some of the techniques used by professionals, parents can, however, create a home environment in which their child can learn and thrive.

Whether one works with a child through the use of discrete trials or through incidental teaching, the terms to remember from this chapter are as follows:

Sd, or **discriminative stimulus** – an instruction stimulating a response from the child. *For example*: 'Put on your hat.'

Reinforcement – anything that, when presented following a behavior, causes that behavior to increase in frequency. *For example*: giving Kara ice-cream after she presents a good report card.

Prompting – assisting the child to ensure that the child's response is correct. *For example*: working David through the act of completing a puzzle with hand-over-hand guidance.

Generalization – exhibiting behaviors and responses which are varied appropriately across a variety of situations. *For example*: When teachers in school ask 'How are you?' Dylan can respond 'I'm fine, thank you,' and when friends in the park ask 'Hey what's up?' Dylan can respond 'I'm cool.'

Shaping – reinforcing successive approximations of a behavior until the entire behavior is mastered. *For example*: Teaching Kara to say 'mmm,' then 'ma' then 'mommy.'

Chaining – teaching a complicated behavior one step at a time. *For example*: Teaching Sara to set the plates on the table, then teaching her to set the plates and the forks, then the plates and the forks and the cups, etc., until she learns to set the entire table by herself.

For each situation that arises in the home and for every interaction, if you begin to ask 'What technique can I apply here to help my child along?' you will begin to form good teaching habits. Practicing using these ideas throughout the day, over time, will help them to become second nature. Once you become adept at applying and practicing these behavioral techniques, formerly difficult tasks and daily activities should run more smoothly and become easier all round. Other ways of applying these techniques will be illustrated throughout this book.

CHAPTER 3

Structuring Your Child's Free Time

Introduction: Why play is an important part of development

All children, at different levels, engage in play activities. These activities are a means of amusement, and help to further the child's development. Despite varying cognitive functioning and language abilities, children with autism can be taught to structure their free time to consist of much play and appropriate engagement.

There are many advantages to teaching children with autism to play appropriately. Children with autism tend to have difficulty interacting with children of their own age in an appropriate and meaningful way. Targeting play enables them to learn the various aspects of appropriate peer interaction. It is also beneficial to the family when these skills are generalized and siblings can become involved. When play skills are practiced with siblings, opportunities for socialization are broadened and can then be generalized to other settings.

Children with autism tend to have a difficult time at community gatherings such as the playground, family holidays and birthday parties. A lack of understanding can preclude a child from participating in an activity and from having the means by which to gain attention and communicate properly. If he learns to participate in a group game or activity, he will be less likely at that time to be engaging in inappropriate behavior, be it self-stimulatory or attention-seeking. Teaching play will enable the child to be a part of the occasion rather than need additional attention and individualized structure.

When leisure time is provided without any activities available, it can be very difficult to manage. Parents often note that they have difficulty talking on the telephone, preparing a meal, or engaging in anything that potentially takes their attention away from their child. In these situations, tantruming as well as a child's perseverative behaviors tend to increase and frustration kicks in. Parents and children alike need leisure time. Providing and teaching skills for leisure and recreation allows this time to be more productive both for the child and for the caregiver.

Play is also a welcome, functional way of gaining another individual's attention and interacting meaningfully. Siblings can begin to strengthen their emotional connection to each other by playing together. Sharing play time can also help to diffuse the difficulty in communication that can be frustrating in building a parent–child relationship.

Finally, there are many skills that children with autism need to practice constantly if these skills are to become a part of their repertoire. Game-playing can become a functional way of practicing mastered skills with a companion. When skills are practiced and introduced through play, learning becomes less routine and more natural. Less resistance is exhibited as task presentation is varied and learning becomes more fun.

In summary, it is important to be able to structure a child's free time for a variety of reasons:

- because it is age appropriate
- to increase interaction with peers and siblings
- to reduce maladaptive behaviors in inclusion settings (the playground, birthday parties)
- to provide skills for leisure and recreation time
- to increase appropriate sociability
- because it can help build positive relationships

- as an appropriate means of gaining attention
- as a functional way of practicing mastered skills with a peer
- as a new way of task presentation: to teach essential skills and educational tasks.

Game playing based on level of functioning

Assessing functional play levels can ensure that children are taught age-appropriate skills and sociability. All children progress through the same stages with regard to their play. Six stages of play based on the child's level of functioning are identified as follows:

1. Object manipulation / isolated play

Object manipulation refers to learning how to manipulate a toy appropriately and independently. This type of play is also called isolated play because here the child engages in object manipulation without a companion.

2. Parallel play

Once a child is able to manipulate a number of toys appropriately, he can be taught to do so alongside a companion. In a parallel play situation, although the children are playing in close proximity to one another, each child is manipulating his own, separate toy.

3. Cooperative play

Cooperative play is an extension of parallel play in which the children involved begin to share materials. An example of this is having two children coloring in a big coloring book and sharing the crayons. Another example is when the children work together on completing a floor puzzle.

4. Turn-taking

Turn-taking is a form of cooperative play which includes an acute awareness that one is playing with another individual. It necessitates waiting for one's turn as well as sharing the materials.

5. Group games

Group games can either be taught once turn-taking has been established, or can be used as a means of teaching turn-taking. Some group games, such as musical chairs, do not require turn-taking at all. In this type of play, the number of individuals interacting is expanded to include more than two.

6. Pretend play

Pretend play is the use of imagination in order to demonstrate the functions of objects, emotions, and/or attributes. Feeding teddy bears and dolls with a toy tea-set is a popular pretend play scenario. Dressing up and playing house or school is another. Even pushing a train along a track and imitating the noise made by the whistle can be considered pretend play. Although pretend play is the most cognitively advanced of the game playing stages, it may emerge along with, or even prior to, some of the other play stages.

Children with autism tend to exhibit splinter skills. A child may have difficulty with language, for example, but easily complete a puzzle beyond her assumed capacity. For this reason one should never assume, when evaluating a child's level of functioning with regard to play activity, that a skill has been mastered simply because a more advanced skill has been exhibited. Each and every type of play within the hierarchy is an important part of development and should be taught, even if more advanced stages have already emerged. The hierarchy is a good method of evaluating a child's development and of guiding a child through activities in as even a progression as possible.

Assessing requisite skills

One of the important steps that needs to be taken before a decision is made as to whether or not a particular activity is appropriate for a child is to assess requisite skills for that activity. If a child is unable to perform a requisite skill, she will be unable to perform the selected activity, and teaching the activity will prove frustrating and become aversive to the child. Identified skills, however, need not necessarily be taught as a prerequisite. Once one is aware that a skill is necessary to an activity, the skill can be taught by focusing on that skill and reinforcing it throughout play time. This detailed focus provides important feedback to the child and encouragement to the parent as individual skills improve.

Skills to target include the following (Note that some of the skills overlap with some of the levels of game-playing already outlined. Other skills are not a specified stage, but rather show up in a variety of activities and play situations.):

- attending
- object manipulation
- motor skills
- turn-taking
- observational learning/ imitation skills
- direction-following
- conditional direction-following
- choice-making
- sharing
- sportsmanship
- initiating play
- appropriate social commenting
- generalization.

It is necessary to look at these skills in further detail before delving into methods of instruction.

Attending

Attending is a skill usually practiced in a one-on-one setting. Targeting attending in a group setting, however, is important for generalization purposes. A child will be able to focus better and learn so much more if he is able to attend even in highly distracting situations such as a group activity. In addition to vastly increasing learning opportunities, this skill can serve as an important social skill and spark further functional interaction. It is important to teach a child to maintain his attention throughout a single activity, thus increasing time on-task, and to switch his attention from activity to activity, thus enabling him to structure his free time with less resistance to change.

Some suggested games for working on attending skills include: bingo games, Lotto games, 'Penguin Shuffle' (by Milton Bradley), and 'Bopping Bee' (by Fisher-Price Games).

Object manipulation/motor skills

Many new activities become accessible to a child as motor skills are developed. In addition to teaching a child how to play with a particular toy, such as a shape sorter, a xylophone or stringing beads, one must teach the child the motor skills needed for these tasks. Gross motor skills are any large-scale movement of the extremities, and are needed in order to tap on a drum or the aforementioned xylophone. Fine motor skills are more subtle manipulations, such as grasping the shapes properly in order to manipulate the shape sorter, or moving one's fingers deftly enough to string beads.

Some suggested games for working on motor skills include: coloring, stringing beads, ball activities such as throwing and kicking, and 'Perfection' (Milton Bradley).

Turn-taking

Turn-taking, in addition to being a requisite skill for a number of games and activities, can serve to reduce maladaptive behaviors during cooperative play. Instead of tantruming, a child learns to wait and is then naturally reinforced as appropriate play skills increase.

Some suggested games for working on turn-taking skills include: blocks, 'Barnyard Bingo' (by Fisher-Price Games); 'Candyland' (by Milton Bradley); 'Don't Spill the Beans' (by Milton Bradley) and 'Topple' (by Pressman).

Imitation skills

Imitation skills give a child the tool needed for observational learning and thus increase independence. Less one-on-one instruction and individualized attention need be provided for a child who is able to imitate and learn from other individuals in his surroundings. Children who learn to imitate can follow their peers in inclusion settings solely by observation.

Some suggested games for working on imitation skills include: follow-the-leader, play doh, 'Simon' (by Milton Bradley), and blocks.

Direction-following

Direction-following increases compliance and develops cognitive skills. When taught in a play situation, such as a 'Simon says' game, direction-following becomes fun and is met with less resistance. Conditional direction-following is cognitively more difficult. The following statement is an example of conditional direction-following: 'If you are wearing a blue shirt, you may take three steps forward.' Conditional direction following is a large part of the party game 'Mother, may I?', in which the leader stands at one end of the room and the other children stand against the opposing wall. The children take turns asking the leader 'Mother, may 1...' (e.g. take three giant steps forward, jump one jump forward, etc.) and the leader may or may not grant the wish. If the wish is not granted, the leader must issue a different command (e.g. 'No, but you must take one small step back.'). The child who reaches the leader first is the winner. Note that requests and commands may vary in difficulty based on the level of the child.

Some suggested games for working on direction-following include: 'Go Fish' by Fisher-Price Games, 'Simon says', 'red light, green light', and 'Mother, may I?'

To play 'red light, green light' have the leader stand at one end of the room and the other children stand against the opposing wall. The leader turns around, covers his/her eyes and calls out 'Red light, green light, one, two, three.' During this time all the children run towards the leader and then freeze. As soon as the leader finishes the chant he/she turns around and any child seen moving is sent back to the starting point. This continues until one child reaches the leader and wins. Then he/she is the new leader.

Choice-making

Choice-making is a skill that surfaces and can be practiced when engaging in almost any board-game. A child may choose the piece she moves in the game, based on shape, color or object. Sometimes a game itself will require choice-making. This is especially the case with regard to pretend play activities that are enacted in group situations. Often children will ask each other if they want their tea with or without sugar. In the park, a child might have to choose between the swing or the slide. Choice-making increases independence and develops individuality.

Some suggested games for working on choice-making include: follow-the-leader, 'Dizzy Dryer' by Mattel, coloring, and beads.

Sharing

The abilities to cheer friends on, be a good loser, and share toys and materials are qualities appreciated in a friend. They are a crucial first step in understanding others' feelings, and enable children to work and play together, cooperating in a meaningful manner.

Some suggested games for working on sportsmanship include: musical chairs, hot potato, 'Sorry' by Parker Brothers, 'Trouble' by Milton Bradley, and 'Mr. Mouth' by Milton Bradley.

Initiating play

Initiating play can be taught for those activities in which appropriate play has already been established. The ability to initiate allows a child to be more assertive in his social interactions in order to better ensure his independent participation. It allows a child to be active in developing friendships.

When working on initiating, be sure to use games that the child plays competently and enjoys.

Social commenting

For verbal children, appropriate social commenting can be a very important focus when looking at integration into less restrictive environments. Appropriate social commenting includes responding appropriately to others' comments, as well as initiating conversation. Conversational skills that can be taught include offers ('Would you like the red crayon?'), comments ('The paper is on the teacher's desk'), compliments, greetings, suggestions and showoffs ('Look at my picture/new red dress').

Suggested games for working on appropriate social commenting include: coloring, play doh, 'Hungry Hippos' by Milton Bradley, and 'house' or 'tea party.'

Generalization

Generalization is the most important aspect of all skills taught. Children need to be able to use their play skills in a variety of settings and with a variety of individuals in order for the skill to become a functional part of their repertoire.

Isolated play and task completion can be taught using shape sorters, puzzles, pop-up toys, and more. These same toys can be used to teach sharing. Some suggested games for working on sharing also include: car garage and musical instruments.

Some suggested games for working on various academic skills, such as colors, letters, and numbers, matching, body parts, daily living skills, and community workers include: 'Boggle Jr.' by Parker Brothers; 'Hi Ho Cherryo' by Parker Brothers; 'Twister' by Milton Bradley; bingo games, Lotto games; 'Oreo Matching Middles' by Fisher-Price Games; 'Snail's Pace Race' by Ravensburger; 'Mr. Potato Head Pals' by Playskool Games; 'The Mighty Mouth Game' by Super Duper School Company; and 'Eight Spin' and 'See Games' by Media Materials.

Adapting materials

When selecting games for a child, keep in mind that child's individual skills. Teach the part of the game that is appropriate for his or her play level. Slowly, expand to include more rules and game skills. Here are some ideas for adapting materials to fit various needs:

Coloring

Use large crayons that are easy to grip. Coloring books may include simple patterns and shapes.

Puzzles

Different puzzles match a variety of motor skill levels. Puzzles with knobs are easier to grip. Puzzles with smaller pieces can help to develop fine motor skills. Puzzles can be used to teach a variety of play skills as well. They can be used in an object manipulation program or as a turn-taking toy. Floor puzzles can be used for a group play activity.

Stringing

Stringing cards are easy to grasp. Beads come in various shapes and sizes. It might be helpful to give the child a box of beads that is only about a third full and contains only one string. This shortens the task and gives it a clear ending, at which point the child can clean up and move on to the next activity.

Memory

Many companies produce memory games. Select a memory game with pictures or characters that will motivate your child. Begin by using only a few cards at a time. If necessary, select cards that can be easily discriminated from each other.

Lotto

Pictures on lotto cards include colors, numbers, shapes, characters, scenery, words and more. Cards can be selected according to the needs of the individual child, and can also be used to facilitate incidental teaching and learning.

Musical chairs

The children can be taught to walk around the chairs to music and sit when the music stops. Removing a chair can be saved for a later date.

Barnyard bingo (or any bingo game)

Not all colors/chips need to be used in order to play this game. Introduce the game with one or two colors/chips at a time.

'Simon says'

This is a game which can begin as a simple, one-step commands program, adding the words 'Simon says' before each command. Eventually, children can learn to lead the game as well as play. Touching the incorrect body part can be used as the criterion for being 'out' before the children are ready to distinguish between when Simon gave the command and when 'Simon didn't say so.' Once the entire game is learned, sportsmanship can be taught as well.

'Red light, green light'
Verbal children can be taught to play this game in full. Non-verbal children can be taught to run and stop at the proper times, and benefit from this game as well.

Conducting a task analysis

Once you are knowledgeable with regard to the hierarchy of game playing, know which skills to work on and have selected and adapted a toy or game to teach, you are ready to begin thinking about how teaching and learning will occur. Applied behavior analysis works by breaking skills down into their components and teaching them one at a time. In order to decipher the component steps of a game, one must conduct a task analysis. Here is a simple task analysis for the game 'musical chairs':

1.   Child stands when music begins.

2.   Child walks around chairs to music.

3.   Child sits when music stops.

When games become more complicated, conducting a task analysis might not be this easy. For an in-depth list of steps, it is best to actually play the game yourself and write down everything you are doing in the process. Then the steps identified can be taught one at a time.

There are two ways to teach a chain of steps and build a sequence of skills to create a complete game-playing repertoire. One way is by teaching the steps in the order in which they occur. The child is required to do the first step of the sequence independently and is then prompted to complete the sequence, and is reinforced. Next, the first two steps are taught as independent, etc. This is called 'forward chaining' (see p.35).

The second way to chain a sequence is to prompt the child through all steps but the last, and teach this last step as an independent skill. Next, the last two steps are taught independently, etc. This is called 'backward chaining' (see pp. 35–36). The advantage of backward chaining is that it usually helps a child to understand the meaning and function of the sequence more quickly and easily. Then the child is naturally reinforced for his independent act with the completion of the game.

How to teach appropriate play

When teaching games and appropriate play skills to children with autism, it is important to modify the instruction and materials used and to arrange the environment in a manner that is both conducive to learning, and in accordance with the participating children's play level.

Instructional techniques

The two most useful methods of direct instruction are prompting and reinforcement. A prompt is used in order to elicit a correct response or, in this case, a desired play action. Two types of prompts to use in this type of instruction are *physical* and *gestural*.

A *physical prompt* involves touching the child in order to guide her to perform a task. Although physical guidance appears to be more intrusive, it is much easier to fade, and thus more apt to establish independent actions from the child. For example, if one wishes to teach a child to complete a puzzle, one should physically prompt her with hand-over-hand guidance until the puzzle is complete, and then praise her for good work. Fairly quickly, the child will need only wrist guidance, a tap on the wrist as a reminder to continue, slight guidance of the elbow, and then no prompt at all. In order to further ensure a quick progression toward independence, always prompt from behind. This allows the child to learn to perform even when the prompter is not present.

A *gestural prompt* involves any sort of gesture that signals to the child to perform the desired task. This gesture can be the act of pointing toward an object, such as the puzzle piece, or even a facial expression. Gestural prompts, although seemingly less intrusive, are much more difficult to fade. They are best used in situations where physical prompting is not practical, or when the gestural prompt would occur naturally in the environment. For example, when saying goodbye it is natural to wave as well. This waving serves as a prompt that need not be faded since it will most likely occur in the natural environment. Gestural prompts are also often used to reinforce turn-taking skills.

When prompting a child, be sure to use the least intrusive prompt necessary. This will promote independence in play. Remember, however, that a prompt is only considered a prompt if it is successful. If the prompt is not eliciting the desired action from the child, a more intrusive prompt might be necessary.

Reinforcement should be given at the completion of any activity that one wishes to increase. Reinforcement can be simple verbal praise, as well as edibles, a desired activity or item/tangible, or a song the child enjoys. When reinforcing, remember that what is reinforcing to a parent or a sibling is not necessarily reinforcing to the child being taught. In order for an item to be reinforcing, it must first be desired. If one is not sure what a child desires, assess various items, one at a time. Some children are able to select their own reinforcers. Encourage choice-making throughout the day. If a child is constantly selecting the same reinforcer, encourage variation.

Always pair verbal praise with any tangible or edible reinforcer given to a child. By pairing reinforcers, the less effective one will start to gain reinforcing qualities, i.e. the child will begin to enjoy and even desire the verbal praise in which he previously showed no interest. Furthermore, if a less desired activity is followed by a more desirable one, the same result will occur. Hence, if one wishes to increase a child's interest in block building and knows that the child loves books, allow the child to read books after building with blocks. The chain of events will begin to lead the child towards the blocks more frequently, for he can expect a fun activity to follow.

Arranging the environment

In order to arrange an environment conducive to play, select a play area and set it up with toys in which the child shows interest. Include new toys that are at the child's level, and teach them periodically during the day. It is important to rotate the toys in the play area in order to avoid satiation. The child, rather than getting sick of any one particular toy, will be ensured novelty and excitement as toys are reintroduced. This strategy will also prevent a child from perseverating on any one particular toy or game. Make sure that the toys to which the child has easy access are those she can play with independently. Strategically position the toys: children often play with a toy because it is right in front of them.

Block off the play area in order to reduce distractions and help the child remain on task. Varying the location of the play area will facilitate generalization.

Motivating the child to participate in play activities

If you consider the child's interests, you will be better equipped to provide for motivation and pleasure. Begin a play session by introducing a toy in which the child shows interest. Work on playing for small periods of time, slowly building up to longer periods of appropriate object manipulation. Self-stimulatory behavior can be redirected into a play skill so that it becomes appropriate. Play is a more accepted, popular outlet for lining and stacking behaviors, among others, and can turn an undesirable behavior into an advantageous one that can include peers and even increase sociability.

Examples: lining, stacking, balancing and rolling of objects can be redirected into block building, building tracks with a train set, stacking-games and cars on race tracks.

Various instructional tools

Timers

Timers are often used for play activities which do not have a specified ending, such as play doh, coloring, and train sets. The timer going off signifies to the child that it is time to clean up and move on to another activity. Teach this by physically prompting the child to switch activities when the buzzer is audible. As a result, tantrums during transitions will be reduced, and the child will learn to move from one activity to the next at a nice pace, without perseverating on any one toy.

Scripts

Written scripts are useful for verbal, literate children who are working on spontaneous conversation during group play. Although teaching a pre-written script is not in and of itself spontaneous, it is a first step in establishing appropriate conversation, and tends to generalize easily to other activities. A script may read as follows:

> **Emma**: 'Look at my picture.'
>
> **David**: 'What is it?'
>
> **Emma**: 'I drew a boy.'
>
> **David**: 'I drew a flower.'
>
> **Emma**: 'Flowers are pretty.'
>
> **David**: 'My flower is red.'
>
> **Emma**: 'I have a red dress. David, what is your favorite color?'
>
> **David**: 'Blue,' etc.

In writing a script, keep in mind the child's age. It is often helpful to observe normally developing peers when determining what to include in the scripted conversation. If rehearsed enough, these phrases will be generalized to other situations and become more spontaneous. Furthermore, it has been demonstrated that, over time, some children will begin to insert spontaneous phrases that were not originally a part of the script.

Observational learning with teacher or peer

Play with the child and demonstrate the same activity repeatedly. By ensuring that all family members are demonstrating the same toys and activities in a consistent fashion, one can speed up the learning process.

Video modeling

Video modeling is a type of observational learning. A parent can videotape himself or a peer playing appropriately, including appropriate commenting, such as whistle sounds for a train set and 'Hello' while talking on a toy telephone. If the child focuses well when viewing a screen, the parent is freed to prompt the child from behind to imitate the video. The physical prompt can be quickly faded. Next, the sound can be turned down. Usually the child will then continue to comment independently, varying the comments and adding new play talk. The last step would be to fade the video altogether.

Group instruction

Before beginning a group instruction, it is effective to teach the target activity one-on-one with an instructor, then by pairing two peers, and only then move on to perform the activity in a group. Once in the group, select one or two specifically defined goals to work on at a time, based on the needs of the individual child. This will make group time less overwhelming and progress easier to track. Different goals can be targeted for different children within the same group. For example, when playing memory, one child can be focusing on matching skill, another child on turn-taking, and a third on memory.

Schedules

A schedule provides a child with structure and an order to his day, leading him from one play activity to the next, without needing further guidance or assistance. Schedules can be written or pictorial, depending on the needs of the child.

To create a schedule, place the label and/or picture of an activity the child can complete independently and enjoys on the front page of a picture album. On the following page, place a representation of a reinforcer. Tell the child to do his schedule. Prompt the child to open the album to the first page, retrieve the materials for the activity, complete the activity and return the items to their original place in the room. Then, prompt the child to turn to the next page of the album, and retrieve the reinforcer. Use physical prompts only, promoting independence. If any verbal prompting accompanies the schedule, the child is no longer playing on his own. Once this pattern is established without any prompting whatsoever, add an activity to the schedule. Be sure to add activities one at a time, before the representation of the reinforcer. A reinforcer should always be at the end of the schedule.

Conclusion

Play is a very important part of a child's development. In order to help structure a child's free time to include appropriate play activity, it is important to understand the various functional play levels through which children progress, and to be able to assess the individual child's play level. When selecting a game or activity, keep in mind the skills needed to perform that activity as well as the child's skills and background. Remember that almost any game can be modified to fit a child's particular needs and abilities. Conduct a task analysis, and proceed to teach the game or activity step by step, using the various instructional techniques illustrated in this chapter.

Before implementing a play program with a child, one should ask oneself the following questions: 'Did I…':

1. assess requisite skills? (This includes observing the child with various selected toys or games.)

2. identify the child's level of play?

3. define specific play goals?

4. select and modify appropriate materials?

5. complete a task analysis?

6. select appropriate instructional methods?

7. assess reinforcers? (Assessing reinforcers ensures that the child enjoys them. Only then will the reinforcer serve to increase a desired behavior.)

8. create a data sheet or tracking device? (Tracking progress ensures objectivity and can help to encourage both the child and the individual implementing the play program.)

9. think of ways to work towards generalizing the skills mastered?

10. have realistic expectations?

If expectations exceed the results, it is no fault of the child nor of the parent. In this case, review the goals, and break them down into simpler steps. Redefining the goals targeted will allow the child to learn at a pace individualized and specially selected to ensure his success.

CHAPTER 4

Reducing Maladaptive Behaviors

Introduction: The benefits of reinforcement over punishment

Maladaptive behaviors are perhaps the most difficult for a parent to deal with on a daily basis. These behaviors can include self-stimulatory, stereotyped movements, tantrums, aggressive and even self-abusive attempts. Instinct tells a parent to punish a child who misbehaves. Punishment, however, has some drawbacks that cause this method to be less than effective when trying to reduce unwanted behaviors for children with autism.

In order for punishment to be successful, it needs to be presented after each occurrence of the behavior being discouraged. Otherwise, instances arise when the behavior is not punished and the child is able to get away with engaging in it. This will almost inevitably lead to another attempt at the behavior, especially in situations of self-stimulatory behaviors which are sensorially reinforcing. It also means that all individuals caring for the child must be able to apply the specific punishment procedure consistently in order for it to be effective.

Punishment can be easy to administer and quick to change a behavior, even if it is not as effective long-term, so that parents who use punishment may find themselves resorting to it more frequently. Punishment has the potential to be overused and abused.

Punishment is not always understood by the child and can elicit fear and aggressive behavior. It can also cause the punisher to be associated with the punishment, and then this fear and aggression become evident in the punisher's presence, even when a punishment is not being delivered.

Children learn from imitation. A child may imitate a punishment and act out towards himself or his peers by imitating the punishment procedure.

Last, punishment must take place immediately following the target behavior. If the behavior occurs and punishment is postponed until father returns home or until mother is free to implement it, the child may not necessarily remember why he is being punished. Even if he is able to remember the reason for the punishment, at this point, the punishment has been weakened in its power to reduce the undesirable behavior. Furthermore, if, by then, the child has engaged in a more suitable, desirable behavior, the punisher will probably reduce that behavior instead of the targeted behavior.

Most importantly, punishment, even if it does work in stopping a behavior which is undesirable, does not establish any new behavior. The emphasis in reducing maladaptive behavior should be to teach children a more appropriate way to achieve their desires. When focusing on reducing maladaptive behaviors, it is important to select a strategy that is not only easy to implement, but that also allows the child many opportunities to learn a positive behavior and to be reinforced with praise and approval every time that new behavior occurs.

Before deciding that a particular behavior is maladaptive and needs to be targeted, remember that all individuals will engage in habits that can be unpleasant and irritating to others. Examples of such behaviors are nail-biting and knuckle-cracking. Although these habits are unattractive, it is not appropriate to use behavioral methods to reduce these behaviors in others.

Guidelines for selecting a behavior to reduce are as follows:

- Is the behavior harmful to the individual engaging in it (self-abusive behaviors)?

- Is the behavior harmful to others (aggression)?

- Does the behavior interfere with learning?

○ Does the behavior restrict the individual's access to the community?

Once a behavior is identified, it can usually be reduced without the use of punishment, and more appropriate behaviors can be established in its place.

Some factors to which maladaptive behaviors may be attributed

1. Environmental conditions

Perhaps the environment is uncomfortable, and the individual is not equipped with the communication skills needed to change the situation. If the behavior is observed in certain rooms but not in others, one may wish to examine the temperature in the rooms and see if that is having an effect on the child. Perhaps the behavior occurs when the child is distracted or confused (*for example*: Tony spins in circles in rooms with detailed wallpaper, and Lee tantrums in new surroundings). Physical demands may also be a factor. For example: a child may become upset when it is demanded of him that he walk. In this case, one may wish to examine his legs and physical strength prior to setting up an intervention program.

2. Medical / physiological causes

Again, a child with an orthopedic need may not be equipped to walk for long periods of time. Also, children who repeatedly bang their heads, hit their ears, or pull on their hair may have earaches. Teeth-clenching may or may not be a result of toothaches. Often, tantrums are indicative of stomach and digestive difficulty. The first step, before beginning an intervention program, should always be to ensure that a child's medical needs are met.

3. Task variables

Sometimes children are simply pushed too hard. It is important always to keep in mind a child's abilities and level of frustration.

Pushing a child may result in more learning, but pushing a child beyond his limit will only bring disaster and anxiety to everyone involved. Allow a tired child nap time. Do not expect her to perform a task that is too difficult for her without proper instruction and prompting. Sometimes, let her be successful at an alternative task when the original task is not reaping her any reward, and then return to the task that is difficult. For example: if a child is not yet able to write properly, write for a few minutes with him, switch to an activity in which he is capable of success, such as reading or puzzles, and then return to the writing. This will both ensure that the child is not bored with one activity, and that he does not learn to hate an activity which he finds difficult. Finally, make sure that the demand placed on him is functional. Set the table with him immediately before mealtime, and work on undressing at bedtime.

Behaviors may also serve functions that are not as easily identified or treated as the ones above. In order to reduce such behaviors, a specific, thought-out plan must be developed and followed consistently by all family members in every situation in which the behavior occurs. This consistency will increase the effectiveness of the plan selected. Note that the following are some common functions of maladaptive behaviors that need to be identified before any plan can be devised and implemented.

4. Self-stimulation

Self-stimulatory behaviors are repetitive motor mannerisms which include grimacing, hand-regarding, hand-flapping, tapping, body-rocking, body-arching, head-rolling, pacing, eye-gazing, vocalizations, and more. These actions, when engaged in repeatedly, provide sensory stimulation, though it is not always clear what sense is being stimulated. For example: hand-flapping could be a motor stimulation, or it could be visual if the child is also gazing at his hands when flapping them. Due to the sensory input provided by these mannerisms, self-stimulatory behaviors are the most difficult to reduce. They provide internal reinforcement that competes with the external reinforcement that could be provided.

5. Attention-seeking

Often behaviors are attention-seeking. A child wishes to gain or regain the attention of an adult and engages in maladaptive behaviors in order to do so. Sometimes a behavior may begin as a self-stimulatory behavior or a medically related one and gradually become attention-seeking. *For example:* June bangs her head on the wall and, as a result, her earache is alleviated. Head-banging becomes associated with comfort and begins to gain self-stimulatory qualities. As soon as mother hears June bang her head on the wall, she comes running into the room to protect and love her daughter. She gives June a hug, and rocks her, repeating the soothing words 'My baby, my sweet darling.' This consequence is very reinforcing for June. June continues her head-banging.

6. Escape/avoidance

All individuals will engage in certain behaviors in order to escape or avoid undesirable activities. One often finds oneself answering the telephone in the middle of washing the dishes and not returning to the dishes once the telephone conversation has ended, or straightening the livingroom as an excuse to avoid doing the accounting. Children will engage in similar escape and avoidance behaviors. One child may break a dish in order to escape the task of clearing the table, and most children try to avoid doing their homework. Children with autism may use maladaptive behaviors more frequently in order to escape an uncomfortable situation or avoid a difficult task.

Each of the above functions is treated in a different fashion. In order to reduce a maladaptive behavior, one must first understand the function that behavior serves. This is, at times, not a simple task. A behavior may appear to be serving one function when in actuality it is serving another, as illustrated in the example of the girl who would bang her head against the wall. In order to discern exactly what is causing and maintaining a behavior, one needs to look at the behavior through the ABC functional analysis model.

ABC functional analysis model

The ABC functional analysis model works to identify the cause of a behavior by exploring the behavior's antecedent and consequence. The first step in analyzing a behavior through this model is to select a behavior (keeping in mind the above guidelines) and clearly define that behavior as specifically as possible.

1. Behavior

A behavior is an action that can be described in great detail. The more specific one is in defining a behavior, the easier it is to work on that behavior. Take the following example: Mother has difficulty with Sarah because Sarah does not pay attention. Although this seems like a behavior one can work on, it is very unclear exactly what Sarah is expected to do. Lack of attention is very difficult to measure. Does it mean that Sarah is not maintaining eye contact? Does it mean that she does not comply with instructions and demands made on her? Or does it mean that she is not noticing that dinner is being served/ father came home from work/the laundry needs folding, etc? Defining Sarah's behavior in more specific terms and providing more detail will allow her mother to plan for small steps of progress comprehensible to Sarah and easily measured. The following chart illustrates how general statements regarding behavior can be more specifically defined:

Table 4.1	
General statements	*Specifically defined behaviors*
X does not attend.	X looks away when spoken to.
X tantrums.	X shouts out and stamps his feet.
X runs away all the time.	X runs away in the supermarket.
X is aggressive.	X kicks and pinches.

2. Antecedent

An antecedent is defined as anything that occurs immediately prior to the behavior's onset. *For example:* company came to visit. Sarah started to tantrum. Once a behavior is clearly defined, it is important to take note of the antecedent whenever the behavior is observed. Studying the antecedent to a behavior usually provides much insight as to the initial cause of the behavior. In this case, perhaps the attention of the members of the household was shifted away from Sarah and toward the company, leading to a tantrum on Sarah's part.

3. Consequence

The consequence refers to anything that follows the behavior. *For example:* Sarah cried loudly, mother gave Sarah a cookie. Although the antecedent originally sparks the behavior, the consequence of the behavior can serve to maintain it. If every time Sarah cries loudly she receives a cookie, she will probably cry more often. By being aware of the consequences one makes for certain behaviors, and of their effect on those behaviors, one can be careful to react in ways that have a long-term positive effect on a child's behaviors and responses to uncomfortable situations.

Conducting a functional analysis

In order to conduct a functional analysis, post a simple chart in an area that is easily accessible. If the child tantrums at bedtime, post the chart on the wall in the bedroom. If leaving the house is difficult for the child, post it near the front door. If mealtime is the issue, post it in the dining-room, etc. The chart should include four columns: one for the time of day when the behavior is observed, one for the ante-cedent, one for an exact and specific description of the behavior, and one for the consequence.

As soon as the behavior occurs, fill in the time of day on the chart. The rest of the columns can be completed after the child has been taken care of and the parent is free to do so. After a week or so, depending on the frequency of the behavior, study the chart, and you should be able to see a pattern forming.

Table 4.2			
Time	Antecedent	Behavior	Consequence

There are other types of charts used for conducting task analyses, but this one is usually the easiest to implement in a home setting. Other behavior-tracking charts include frequency charts, which track how often a behavior occurs, duration charts, which track how long a behavior lasts, and more. Tracking behaviors allows one to begin to detect and understand the pattern of a behavior, or the chain of events causing/maintaining it, and is very helpful in reducing it.

Proactive strategies

Using the 'antecedent–behavior–consequence' (ABC) method, one can manipulate antecedents and consequences in a systematic way in order to change behaviors. Proactive strategies are strategies that manipulate or alter the antecedent that signals that the behavior is about to occur. Proactive strategies reduce a maladaptive behavior by preventing the behavior from occurring before it has started. There are a variety of ways in which this can be accomplished:

Environmental changes

Changing the environment may, at times, be enough to prevent an unwanted behavior from occurring. *For example:* if Billy runs around in circles to one specific Barney tape only, but enjoys other music as well, do not play that tape. If Donna licks the red fire-truck, let her play with the police car and the school bus and only introduce the fire-truck for brief periods of supervised time. If Robby cries when the alphabet puzzle is taken away and climbs on the shelves in the closets looking for it, throw it out. This is not meant as a punishment, but is a way of helping a child to expand his tastes calmly and happily without being distracted and upset by an overstimulating toy, which can later be reintroduced.

Changing the environment, however, is not always the solution. If Robby cries for all puzzles, he needs to learn to play with them and then let go. One cannot create a situation in which a child listens to no music at all, or in which manipulating the environment becomes cumbersome to family and friends.

Changes in routine

There are many children who have difficulty either adapting to or changing an established routine. Even adults are upset when their day does not go as expected. This becomes more potent an issue for children with autism, who might not yet be at the stage of concept formation that allows them to understand that a small change does not necessarily mean complete instability. Practicing routines within the home allows children to learn what to expect from their day and allows for easier transitioning from activity to activity. Routines can include a morning bathroom and dressing time, a lunchtime in which the child works through hand-washing and table-setting, a bedtime routine with a story and hugs, etc. Paying close attention to routines in the home allows one to take notice of which parts of the day a child finds upsetting. Some change and instability can, indeed, be eliminated. *For example:* in school Lisa may be allowed to expect lunch every day after group-time, and dinner every day at six. If this is not a realistic expectation in Lisa's household, perhaps she may be able to anticipate bathtime to be always immediately following dinner. Some change, however, is inevitable, and it is important that children learn to deal with change that will occur throughout their lives.

When working with a child on adapting to change, be sure to precede the change with a warning. Any child who understands that change is about to take place is better equipped to handle the feelings that go along with it. Furthermore, do not expect a child to adapt to many changes at once. Decide on one alteration, and work on it. Then add another. *For example*: if John tantrums unless the bathroom door is closed, the dining-room chairs are touching each other and his toy chest is as he left it, do not disrupt everything at once. First, open the bathroom door and do not close it as a result of his tantruming. After he has adapted nicely to the door being open or shut, then work on either the chairs or the toy chest. It is important not to relinquish all decisions with regard to a child's environment to the child, because otherwise he will be unable to function outside his own home setting. However, it is helpful to keep in mind the child's needs and sensitivities when working with him on tolerating change.

Teaching adaptive communication skills

The most important tool a child has to help him adapt to any difficult or uncomfortable situation is communication. By teaching adaptive communication skills, you enable your child to obtain food when he is hungry, warmth when he is cold, medication when he is sick, and love and attention when he feels lonely. With these needs met, fewer maladaptive behaviors will surface.

Children do not need to be verbal in order to communicate. To establish adaptive communication skills, review all the types of conventional communication illustrated in Chapter Six.

The following is an example of a functional analysis in which proactive strategies were used and communication skills established in order to reduce a maladaptive behavior:

Behavior: Timmy repeatedly climbed on the refrigerator.

Antecedent: Although the antecedent in this case was not recorded by the parent, the parent noted that Timmy would try to retrieve the food that was stored above the refrigerator whenever he was hungry.

Consequence: Mother fed Timmy.

In this scenario, Timmy was being reinforced for climbing the refrigerator. In essence, he was being taught that climbing the refrigerator will result in obtaining food. In order to alter this chain of events, some suggestions were made to the mother. Whenever Timmy climbed, he was to be brought down and led to the place in the room where he had previously been standing. Then he was to be prompted to tap his mother on the arm and request food (in Timmy's case, this request was made verbally). His mother was then immediately to give him something to eat. This way, Timmy learned a more functional and effective way of letting his hunger be known and satisfied. After a couple of weeks, the prompt was no longer needed. (Note that the reason for bringing Timmy back to the place where he was originally standing in the room was to ensure that the chain of events leading to his receiving food was appropriate. Instead of reinforcing a chain of behaviors in which Timmy climbs, requests, and receives food, Timmy's mother was advised to teach him that he must request from the spot where he decided he was hungry, and then give him the food as a response to his request. The food served as a natural reinforcer.)

Differential reinforcement of other behaviors (DRO)

Differentially reinforcing other behaviors is very simple. It consists of remembering to reinforce the child for 'being good.' Whenever the child is not engaging in the maladaptive behavior, let him know that he is doing a good job. It is important, however, not to refer to the maladaptive behavior in the reinforcement. By saying something like 'You are not flapping your hand, I like that,' one is only calling attention to the behavior one wishes to reduce. Rather, praise the child for a positive action: 'Your hands are in your lap and you are listening so nicely!' This way, no attention is received for the maladaptive behavior, and a positive behavior is reinforced in its place. By taking the specifically defined behavior from the ABC functional analysis and reversing it, one can create behavior-specific verbal reinforcement and praise:

Table 4.3	
Behavior defined	*Behavior-specific reinforcement*
X looks away when spoken to.	I like the way you are looking at me!
X shouts out and stamps his feet.	Wow! You are being so quiet!
X runs away in the supermarket.	Nice waiting!
X kicks and pinches.	Good job keeping your hands to yourself!

Reactive strategies

Reactive strategies are ones that manipulate or alter the consequence of a behavior. Behaviors that are followed by pleasant consequences are more likely to happen again. Behaviors that are not followed by pleasant consequences are not likely to happen again. It is important to keep in mind here that what a child may conceive as a pleasant consequence may be very different from an adult's preconceived notion of what reinforcement is and should be. Take, for example, a child who does not complete his homework and is constantly being lectured to by his father. The father sees his long lectures as a verbal punishment, whereas the child may enjoy the attention he receives from the father during these lecture episodes. This is especially the case in a situation where the father is a busy, working man and does not have time to provide his son with positive attention. Even negative attention can be positively reinforcing.

1. Extinction

Extinction is the act of selectively ignoring a behavior. This way, a child does not receive any reinforcement for a maladaptive behavior. Extinction cannot be used for self-injurious behaviors. Also, remember that extinction never means ignoring a child completely.

While the maladaptive behavior is ignored, differential reinforcement of other, more appropriate behaviors should take place. Furthermore, extinction is usually not enough, when implemented in isolation from other techniques, to reduce an unwanted behavior. Other techniques to use in conjunction with extinction include interrupting the behavior, especially if it is self-injurious; redirection; teaching adaptive communication skills, etc. Extinction is an important technique to use for any behavior that is attention-seeking.

2. Interrupting the behavior

Interrupting a behavior is usually a successful method of initially stopping self-stimulations. To interrupt a behavior, gently touch the child in the least intrusive fashion possible while at the same time ensuring a successful interruption. For example, if the child is tapping, place your hand over hers. If she is rocking, place a hand on her shoulder. For verbal self-stimulation, have the child repeat simple verbal imitations, slowly progressing to more complicated verbalizations such as requesting and social questions. Once a behavior is interrupted, a new, more appropriate behavior must be established in its place in order to ensure that the self-stimulation of maladaptive behavior does not immediately return. This can be accomplished by redirecting the child.

3. Redirection

Redirection consists of directing the child to a task where the undesirable behavior is not observed. Usually it is helpful if this selected, new, appropriate behavior is incompatible with the undesirable, maladaptive one. If hand-flapping has been interrupted, redirect the child to a coloring activity. If extraneous verbalizations have been interrupted, redirect the child to sing. If rocking behavior has been interrupted, redirect the child to an activity which includes walking, running or dance. Try to redirect quickly and quietly. Remember that even when redirecting, the child should receive as little attention as possible until the more appropriate behavior has already been established.

4. Sensory extinction

Sensory extinction is used in order to remove or lessen the sensory input gained from engaging in the behavior. It is also often used as protection from self-injurious behavior. Note that a child who is pulling on his ears on a continuous basis and has been examined to reveal no internal infections may benefit from a headphone set. Headphones may provide the child with the same sensations gained from ear-pulling, while being both appropriate and safe.

Examples of behavior plans for frequently asked questions

(Note that these are examples of suggestions given to specific parents and specific children. They will not necessarily prove successful for every child who engages in a behavior similar to one described in any of the questions. Plans need to be individualized according to the guidelines illustrated in this chapter.)

My child runs away in the supermarket, what should I do?

First, teach the child to respond to his name by having him call back 'What?' His voice will guide you to his location. Also, make it a priority to practice the instruction 'Come here' with a variety of people and in a variety of settings. It is very important to guarantee that the child will respond to this instruction one hundred percent of the time. This means that whenever you call the child to you, you must follow through and make sure that he comes (physically prompt if necessary) the first time you call him. Practically, this means that you should only call your child when you are at leisure to go get him (i.e. not when you are in the middle of doing the dishes and are aware that he will not respond and that you will not follow through).

Responding to any one instruction is always more difficult if one is already engaging in another behavior that is incompatible with the instruction. For this reason, teach your child 'Stop' and 'Go.' If the child is running, first say 'Stop,' and once he has stopped it should be easier for him to respond appropriately to the instruction 'Come here.' 'Stop' and 'Go' can be taught as a Freeze Tag game with siblings and peers, so that it is fun, reinforcing, and more easily learned.

Use these instructions consistently in all environments. Although adults know that it is safe to run in a park but not in a store, a child may not be able to make that distinction.

Finally, engage the child in the shopping process. Supermarkets are wonderful places to practice verbal skills, pointing, choice-making, labels (receptive and expressive, for example: 'Show me the banana') and other crucial skills. By allowing your child to select one item per aisle, or otherwise participate in the grocery shopping, you can teach and interact. Engaging your child in the shopping activity will also provide him with reinforcement from you for being appropriate and possibly prevent him from running in the first place.

My child is constantly flipping through the pages of all the books in the house, what should I do?

First, set down some rules, and stick to them. By doing so, you are not being cruel. You are providing structure that all children need in order to learn how they are expected to behave. The bookcase in the family room with valuable books that other members of the family read can be off-limits. That means that whenever the child approaches that bookcase, he is redirected to a bookcase designated for him with children's books and/or magazines. Although this will be a difficult rule to implement, the child should quickly learn which books he may read and which he may not.

Next, physically prompt him to take only one book from the shelf at a time. Before taking a new book to read, prompt him to return the one in his hands. Finally, take some time out every day to read with him. During this time, prompt him to stay on each page for one second before flipping to the next. After this becomes natural to him, begin to work on two seconds, etc. If the books have pictures, this is a good time to work on object and activity recognition (also forcing the child to remain on one page for longer periods of time).

My child spits, what should I do?

It is crucial, before deciding on a plan, to track when the spitting occurs and what function it is serving. For spitting that is attention-seeking, ignore the spitting, while teaching and reinforcing a more appropriate way of asking for attention.

For spitting that is serving the function of getting out of a task (escape/avoidance), ignore the spitting while working the child through the task. In this case, you may also wish to teach the child a more appropriate way of asking for a break or saying no to a request or demand that is placed on him.

If the spitting is self-stimulatory, first disengage the child by implementing verbal imitations (see Chapter Six) and other verbal responses. Spitting is incompatible with talking and should therefore stop. Be very careful not to address the spitting directly, because this can inadvertently add reinforcement as a maintaining factor. If the sense that is being stimulated by the behavior is that of sight, perhaps a kaleidoscope will provide the same sensory input. If the sense being stimulated involves the tongue and the mouth, perhaps a candy will provide the sensory input sought by the child. Remember that self-stimulatory behavior increases when a child has no other activity in which to engage. For long car or bus rides, give the child a book or a toy to bring along. (Note that even an inappropriate toy may become more appropriate if it serves to reduce spitting behavior.)

Conclusion

All plans should be implemented in conjunction with DRO (differentially reinforcing other behavior). Children need to learn not only how not to misbehave, but also how to behave. It is crucial that one does not halt a child's means of communication and of reacting to her surroundings without providing her with an alternative outlet and means of communication. Plans that have been designed carefully to fit an individual child's needs, that are consistent and practical, and that are taught in conjunction with alternate, positive behaviors, are more likely to be successful.

A behavior plan will not ensure that the maladaptive behavior will disappear overnight. You need to be practical in deciding what you can implement, and the gains that you expect to see. Always be prepared for a behavior to get worse before it gets better. This is because new demands are being placed on the child, and it takes time for her to learn how to respond to them. Remember that even if the maladaptive behavior does increase when first treated, it will probably decrease over time. If a plan has been implemented for a while, however, and is indeed not successful, you may simply wish to re-examine the function of the child's behavior and re-evaluate the plan. Perhaps a different plan will work better to decrease the behavior and increase appropriateness.

CHAPTER 5

Daily Living Skills

Introduction: Helpful hints on increasing your child's independence

It is difficult for any parents to find the fine line between helping their child in an immediate situation, and allowing the child to learn independence by struggling with a daily living skill. Children with autism who are allowed to work independently rather than taught to rely on parental assistance are better able to function in the home and in other community settings. The earlier independence is demanded of a child, the easier it will be for him to learn the necessary skills for daily self-care and management.

Children need to be given the opportunity to struggle with tasks such as self-dressing, hand-washing, routine cleaning, self-feeding, and even having to stay alone at bedtime and falling asleep. This does not mean that parents are precluded from caring and from helping their children to learn to adjust to independence and to correctly perform these tasks.

Parents of children with autism and/or other developmental disabilities are in the habit of taking extra care with their children. Although this is sometimes necessary, it is important to remember that all children, including those with autism, can benefit from guided trial and error. Make time for the child to learn to dress himself before leaving the house. Allow for messes at the table when the child learns to eat with a fork. Be prepared for falls and scraped knees when he struggles trying to climb a staircase. Also, keep certain guidelines in mind when trying to lead your child toward independent living and independent accomplishments in the home.

We saw that prompting is the most important teaching tool, in that a prompt ensures that the child will complete a given task correctly. Children with autism can, however, easily become dependent on prompts. In order to increase a child's independence, prompts must be faded as quickly as possible.

Allow a child to work through his frustration for tasks which you know are not beyond his capacity. If a child is able to open the door, do not open it for him. Even if he is having difficulty and asks for help, let him struggle with the task and feel accomplishment when he finally succeeds. Do not teach him to give up quickly. If the child asks for juice, let him pour the juice himself, even though most of the juice may spill. Let him have to reach high shelves on his tippy toes, work a little to remove his shoes and learn to put effort into tasks he will need to learn for life. (Again, be sure that the tasks chosen are not beyond his capacity and that he is guided to success before complete independence is required.)

Establishing a healthy sleeping pattern

All children have nightmares and will wake up late at night and enter their parents' room and bed. Since children with autism may overgeneralize easily, parents of these children may need to be extra careful in establishing bedtime rules and sticking to them. A large number of parents of autistic children report that their children exhibit unusual sleeping patterns, and these parents find themselves and other family members losing sleep. The child herself may even be tired during the day as a result of lack of sleep, and her school work and learning may be affected. Here are some general suggestions for helping your child to establish a healthy sleeping pattern that is more easily manageable.

1. Establish a late bedtime

Instinct has parents putting their children to sleep between seven-thirty and nine-thirty. Children who have difficulty sleeping through the night may simply need a later bedtime. To illustrate: Sal went to sleep at eight o'clock every evening – a reasonable bedtime for an eight-year-old. Every night, at four a.m., his parents found him in the livingroom, jumping on the sofa. By morning, both Sal and his parents were exhausted. It was suggested that Sal's bedtime be moved to eleven-fifteen. After a period of adjustment, Sal got the same number of hours of sleep as he did with the nine-thirty bedtime, only now he would wake up at six a.m., and he and his parents were able to function during the day without feeling as tired.

2. Allow the child to bring a preferred item to bed

Often a child will not go to sleep because he wants to read his book or hold his Barney doll, pick-up truck, etc. Bringing a toy to bed may not be conducive to sleep, but it will make bedtime less aversive. Sometimes, especially if siblings are involved (they share a bedroom, have school or a test the next day, and cannot sleep because of the noise and commotion involved in putting the child with autism to sleep), it is easier and more functional for the family as a unit to reduce the stress of bedtime and work on actual sleeping later.

3. Take a couple of weeks to establish rules and work through tantrums

Ricky's parents decided that Ricky should no longer be allowed in their bed. They understood that they had to break this habit while Ricky was still young, and selected a vacation week to establish that he must remain in his own room throughout the night. Since Ricky was still a child, they decided that it was appropriate for him to wake up at night for a glass of water, and perhaps a hug. When Ricky cried, his parents opened his door to make sure that he was well. They brought him water, sat with him for five minutes, and sang a lullaby. Then they left his room.

Day 1: Ricky cried for an hour and twenty minutes. He tried to open his door, and when he found that it was held shut, he threw himself against it repeatedly, trying to escape. Finally, he tired himself out and fell asleep on the floor.

Day 2: Ricky threw himself against the door, screaming 'Let me out.' He fell asleep after two hours.

Day 3: Ricky threw himself against the door five times and sobbed for an hour, until he fell asleep.

Day 4: Ricky threw himself against the door once, cried for twenty minutes, and went to sleep.

Day 5: Ricky drank his water and fell asleep during his five minute lullaby.

Although this scenario seems cruel, Ricky's parents always went in to make sure that Ricky was not thirsty or sick. They knew that they needed to establish new rules before Ricky grew older.

When deciding to work through a night-time tantrum, make sure to select a time that is convenient for all of the family members involved. Once a rule is set, it needs to be established through consistency. If a rule is not implemented on a consistent basis, it will not become routine. Also, make sure that the child is always safe. Self-abusive behaviors cannot be ignored. In the case of self-injury, alternative plans must be explored. Finally, be prepared for the behavior to get worse before it gets better. Establishing a new routine takes time and patience, and although it is not always easy physically or emotionally, it is effective. For more information on sleeping patterns and disorders, see references from Chapter Ten.

Toilet-training

To begin a toilet-training program, parents need a lot of patience and dedication. Accidents should be expected, and during the program parents must be available to take the child to the bathroom periodically throughout the day. For cases in which a parent or other responsible adult is not available to do so, the parent can work on toileting

Table 5.1 – Data sheet: Toileting

Date	Time	Success	Accident	Request	Comments

for a specified amount of time each day until the child advances and needs a full-day program.

A child who is being toilet-trained should be wearing underwear. This is especially the case for children with autism. Wearing underwear makes accidents more uncomfortable and provides further motivation for the child to learn to use the bathroom appropriately. Also, underwear makes it easier to see that a child needs the bathroom and is about to have an accident (look for bent knees in boys and spread legs in girls). Then you have a better chance of rushing the child to the bathroom in time.

Now that the child is in underwear, bring the child to the bathroom every five to ten minutes, giving him a lot of liquid to drink in the interim. When he successfully urinates on the toilet, reinforce his behavior with social praise and the most potent edible or activity. Make sure that the reinforcer used is available only for the toileting program, as this will increase motivation. As soon as the child is successful on a more consistent basis, this reinforcement can begin to be faded. Although it is usually necessary for the child to sit for only a couple of minutes each time he is brought to the bathroom, there are cases in which the child continues to have accidents. In order to ensure success, after giving the child a lot of liquid, try seating him on the toilet until he is successful. This may take up to an hour, especially if the child is resistant. If necessary, bring a book or music into the bathroom and allow the child to stand every fifteen minutes to prevent leg cramping.

Once a couple of consecutive days of data show that the child is no longer having accidents, increase the time between bathroom visits to fifteen minutes, then twenty, then half-an-hour, etc. If the data at any point show an increase in accidents that cannot be attributed to illness or any other major change in routine (this would be evident when reviewing the comments written on the data sheet), it may be necessary to move back a step and bring the child to the bathroom more frequently. Adding a step is also useful. *For example*: Dana did not have accidents when she was on a half-an-hour toileting schedule. She had many accidents on a forty-five minute toileting schedule over the course of three days. A middle step of thirty-five minutes was instituted, and Dana was able to progress in her toileting program.

Check for other patterns in the data, as well. If a child is having accidents at a particular time of day, perhaps try taking him to the bathroom more often at that time. Children usually need the bathroom in the morning, around lunchtime and after school. Being sensitive to these needs will help a child to toilet-train.

Once a child is no longer having accidents and his toileting schedule is up to a couple of hours between bathroom visits, introduce requesting as part of the program. A child can be taught to request the bathroom verbally, using sign language, or through a picture exchange system. Note that some children are able to skip straight to this step and begin a toilet-training program with a requesting element. These are typically the children who resent being taken to the bathroom on a regular schedule and already understand what the room is for and when they need it.

When working on a toilet-training program, always take the opportunity to teach other related self-help skills such as pulling pants down, pulling pants up, flushing, and washing hands. In order to teach these skills, physically prompt the child through the entire procedure. This will promote independence, for the child will not have an opportunity to become dependent on a verbal prompt. Here is an example of a prompt-dependent teenager:

Will was completely toilet-trained. His parents, however, were in the habit of talking him through the event as follows:

'Zip your pants.'

'Flush the toilet.'

'Good, Will, now turn on the water and wash your hands.'

'You need more soap, Will.'

'Shut off the water.'

'Good, now dry your hands on the towel.'

Will turned fifteen, and still needed these verbal prompts. In fact, one day in school, when these prompts were not provided, Will got very agitated. He knew that he needed to wash his hands, but he would not do so until he heard the prompt. He would not go back to his classroom, either. Although his parents meant well, they did not teach Will to be independent. Physical prompts, although more intrusive, would have been better in the long term (but be careful not to push a child too hard and not to make the program aversive).

Food selectivity and other mealtime issues

Before beginning a program to decrease food selectivity, consider the following:

- ○ Is the child currently working on toilet-training?
- ○ Are there other, more pressing behaviors that need to be addressed?
- ○ Is there a skill deficit involved (i.e. is the child not eating certain foods because he has not developed the muscles needed for chewing or because he cannot hold a fork)?

If the answer to any of these questions is 'yes,' then it is advised that a food selectivity program be postponed. Food selectivity programs are emotionally demanding and, combined with another difficult program, will overwhelm the child so that neither program will succeed.

If the answer to the above questions is 'no,' start to keep a complete running record of the child's diet for anywhere from a few days to a week. This should present you with a fair picture of what exactly needs to be added to his menu. For each meal, record the foods eaten (including the amount of each food, if possible) and the food's texture and consistency. After reviewing the data, you should be able to see a clear pattern with regard to one of the following eating issues:

1. The child will/will not eat foods of a certain texture.

2. The child will/will not eat foods of a certain color.

3. The child will/will not eat foods of a certain taste (sweet, sour, mild, spicy).

Table 5.2 – Dietary log

Date	
Meal	
Foods served	
Foods eaten	
Consistency/ texture	
Comments	

After reviewing the log, select one or two goals. Write the goals down to ensure that they are clear and specifically defined. Remember that the goals selected need to be attainable. In implementing a goal, follow these guidelines:

1. Establish a child's hunger at specific times during the day. A child should be hungry for breakfast, lunch, dinner, and perhaps a snack. Make sure that he has access to food only at these times, and that snacking (other than edible reinforcers used in sessions) is limited so as not to spoil his appetite.

2. Make a list of the child's preferred foods, and limit his intake of these foods.

3. At mealtime, the child will be hungry (see 1). First, serve a small portion of the goal food which he does not like to eat. The portion should fill no more than one quarter of a teaspoon. Make his eating a preferred food conditional upon his eating the goal food. *For example*: Celia will not eat vegetables. She loves to eat pasta. At lunchtime, Celia's mother gives her one bite of broccoli. She also places a plate of spaghetti on the table, and tells Celia, 'Eat your broccoli and then you can have the spaghetti.'

4. Be consistent and follow through. If Celia does not eat the broccoli, her mother may not give her the spaghetti. Celia may have to go without lunch. This will, however, whet her appetite for dinner and increase her motivation to eat the broccoli at that time.

5. Do not continue this program if a child is losing nourishment. In this case, consult with a physician.

6. Slowly increase the amount of non-preferred food that the child is required to eat. The child should begin to find this food less aversive since it is followed by a food he likes.

7. Refrain from offering the child foods he does not enjoy at other times during the day.

There are many skill deficits that can affect mealtime issues. Here are some skills that a child may need help in practicing:

- pincer grasp (using the thumb, pointer and index fingers to lift finger-food and bring it to the mouth)
- spooning
- spearing
- proper use of a fork
- using a knife to cut
- using a knife to spread.

Practicing these skills with preferred food items and when the child is hungry will increase her motivation to learn and succeed in self-feeding. *For example*: if Larry's favorite food is steak, use steak to teach him how to use a fork. Physically prompt him from behind to use his fork properly with each bite. If he does not use his fork the way he should, take that bite off the fork before it gets to his mouth and prompt him to use the fork properly. Being able to eat his favorite food will be enough of a reinforcer, and you should be able to fade the prompt and work toward independent eating.

For children with less developed fine motor skills, see catalogs for specially crafted utensils. Spoons, forks and knives are made for easier grasping with either the right or the left hand. Dishes are made with higher sides to avoid spills and with sections to keep different foods separated.

Some mealtime issues that all parents face concern table manners. If a child is in the habit of picking at his food, avoid using verbal reminders which are difficult to fade. Instead, physically prompt the child to chain a number of bites together. The food itself will be reinforcing, and you can add an occasional compliment such as 'You are eating very nicely.' Slowly increase the number of bites chained together.

Highly verbal children, especially those diagnosed with Asperger's syndrome, may have difficulty concentrating simultaneously on their food and the conversation around the table. Here is how Larry learned to do so:

A timer was placed at the dinner table. Larry set the timer for one minute at the start of dinner. During that minute, he was required to participate in the conversation and eat. If he was successful, he had five minutes to relax as he wished (eat, talk, daydream). If he forgot to eat or forgot to join the conversation at appropriate times, the timer was reset to begin another minute. Once Larry could concentrate at mealtime for one minute consistently, he was told to set the timer for two minutes, and so on.

To increase the time a child spends sitting at the table:

1. Do not follow the child and feed him around the house. When he is hungry enough, even if it takes a full day, he will come to the table.

2. Be prepared to work through tantrums.

3. Do not make mealtime aversive. If a child cannot sit at the table for the entire meal, begin with sitting at the table for one to three bites. Increase the number of bites that the child is required to eat at the table slowly, as small steps are mastered and generalized to a variety of foods.

4. Stop the program and consult a physician if the child is losing nutrition.

5. Serve preferred foods at the table.

Self-dressing

Self-dressing programs can be made functional by practicing them at appropriate times of the day. Since functional programs are most successful, dressing is a practical and useful skill to practice with a child in the home. Included here are task analyses for the following dressing skills:

- taking off and putting on shoes
- taking off and putting on pants
- taking off and putting on shirts
- taking off and putting on coats.

As with games, you can create your own self-dressing task analysis by completing the task and writing down every step involved in its completion. Keep in mind, when working with a child on a self-dressing program, that children usually learn to remove their clothing before they learn to dress independently.

Before beginning a self-dressing program, work on teaching the child to retrieve the item of clothing from the closet. When he removes an item of clothing, practice returning it to its proper place, whether that is the closet or the laundry-basket. If he has extra difficulty with zippers, snaps, buttons or laces, practice these skills independent of the dressing program. Many catalogs sell lacing cards with larger laces, button cards with larger buttons, and snap and zipper cards. Working with these cards should reduce the child's frustration and facilitate dressing later on. Also, assess whether or not he has the motor skills necessary for completing these tasks.

The dressing programs can be taught using either forward or backward chaining. In order to forward-chain a dressing program, follow the steps as they are written in the task analyses. In order to backward-chain a dressing program, follow the steps in reverse order. Backward-chaining is beneficial here in that, for example, a child who begins by learning to zip his coat is ready to go out and play, whereas a child who begins by learning to put on one sleeve still needs be prompted through complete dressing before he can be reinforced. (For a review of forward and backward chaining, see Chapter Two.)

Whenever a child is dressing, work on this program. Begin by physically prompting the entire task analysis. Next, see if the child is able to complete the first step independently. If so, record a (+) in the box for Step 1. If not, record a P (prompt), and continue to teach it. Once the step is mastered and the child can execute it independently (using a variety of shirts if he is working on shirts, a variety of pants if he is working on pants, etc.), see if he can complete Steps 1 and 2 independently, then Steps 1, 2 and 3, and so on. Remember not to prompt verbally.

Table 5.3 – Task analysis for taking off shoes										
Date:										
Step 1: sit down.										
Step 2: hold string with fingers and pull.										
Step 3: loosen tongue of shoe.										
Step 4: place hand on heel of shoe.										
Step 5: pull shoe off.										
Step 6: pull string of other shoe.										
Step 7: loosen tongue of other shoe.										
Step 8: place hand on heel of other shoe and pull shoe off.										

Table 5.4 – Task analysis for putting on shoes

Date:										
Step 1: place shoes on floor.										
Step 2: sit down.										
Step 3: slip foot into shoe, holding the tongue for assistance.										
Step 4: hold heel of shoe.										
Step 5: push foot into shoe.										
Step 6: slip other foot into shoe, holding the tongue of the shoe.										
Step 7: hold heel of shoe and push foot in.										
Step 8: tie shoes.										

Table 5.5 – Task analysis for tying shoes

Date:										
Step 1: make a loop with one string and hold.										
Step 2: make a loop using the other string and your other hand.										
Step 3: twist the loops around each other.										
Step 4: tie the strings in a bow.										

Table 5.6 – Task analysis for taking off pants

Date:										
Step 1: take off shoes (if they are on).										
Step 2: unsnap/un button pants.										
Step 3: unzip pants.										
Step 4: pull pants down.										
Step 5: sit down.										
Step 6: hold bottom cuff of pant leg.										
Step 7: pull pant leg off.										
Step 8: hold bottom of other cuff and pull pant leg off.										

Table 5.7 – Task analysis for putting on pants										
Date:										
Step 1: sit down.										
Step 2: find tag in pants.										
Step 3: use both hands to hold top of pants with tag closer to you.										
Step 4: place foot in pant leg.										
Step 5: pull pant leg up.										
Step 6: place other foot in other pant leg.										
Step 7: pull pant leg up.										
Step 8: stand up.										
Step 9: pull up pants.										
Step 10: zip/snap/ button pants.										

Table 5.8 – Task analysis for taking off shirt										
Date:										
Step 1: hold bottom of sleeve with opposite hand.										
Step 2: pull arm out of sleeve.										
Step 3: hold bottom of other sleeve with opposite hand.										
Step 4: pull arm out of sleeve.										
Step 5: put both hands on bottom of shirt.										
Step 6: pull shirt over head.										

Table 5.9 – Task analysis for putting on shirt									
Date:									
Step 1: find tag in shirt.									
Step 2: place shirt on lap, with tag on top.									
Step 3: put head in shirt.									
Step 4: pull shirt over head.									
Step 5: put arm in sleeve.									
Step 6: pull sleeve up over hand.									
Step 7: put other arm in other sleeve.									
Step 8: pull sleeve up over other hand.									
Step 9: use both hands to pull shirt down so that it covers body.									

Table 5.10 – Task analysis for taking off coat

Date:										
Step 1: pull off hood (if necessary).										
Step 2: unzip coat.										
Step 3: pull bottom of sleeve with opposite hand.										
Step 4: take arm out of coat-sleeve.										
Step 5: pull bottom of other sleeve with opposite hand.										
Step 6: take arm out of coat-sleeve.										

Table 5.11 – Task analysis for putting on coat

Date:										
Step 1: hold coat facing you.										
Step 2: extend arm diagonally across your body.										
Step 3: put arm in sleeve.										
Step 4: pull coat over your shoulder, using opposite hand.										
Step 5: put your other arm in other sleeve.										
Step 6: zip coat.										
Step 7: put on hood (if necessary).										

Conclusion

Promoting independence is the only way to teach a child the skills needed for survival beyond parental care. Looking toward a child's future and preparing for his self-care at a young age is the best gift a parent can give him. It makes life more pleasant for the child, adds to his sense of accomplishment and frees the parent for other parental activities.

Over time, independence also allows a child to further develop her skills as these skills are applied to new situations. A child who is proficient at making her own sandwich for lunch should, eventually, be able to vary the sandwich's ingredients independently as new ones are made available. A child who knows how to put on a jacket and how to button his pants should be able to put on his dress shirt with little practice.

Physically prompting children through self-care tasks such as dressing, washing, and cleaning up toys, while fading these prompts as quickly as possible, will help to increase independence. Healthy sleeping patterns, toilet-training and mealtime appropriateness should be established at a young age, following the guidelines illustrated in this chapter.

Schedules can also be used as tools to help increase a child's independence. Written schedules can be posted to facilitate bedtime routines. For example:

1. The clock reads 8:00.

2. Put on pajamas.

3. Go to bathroom and brush teeth.

4. Read book.

5. Shut off light and go to sleep.

Picture schedules can be posted to help facilitate bath and shower time. For example: on the wall in the shower, post a picture of soap and a picture of a washcloth. Then post pictures of all the body parts in the order that the child is to wash them. Physically prompt the child through this sequence, having her point to the picture and wash the body part which she pointed to, etc. Once she is proficient at this, the pictures can remain on the wall of the shower as reminders, and parental assistance will no longer be needed.

CHAPTER 6

Increasing Communication

Introduction: Establishing realistic goals for your child

Communication is the act of transmitting information by means of a common system. Conventional systems include speech, sign language, picture-exchange systems, written communication, Morse code, and more.

Children with autism usually exhibit difficulty in their communication skills. Typically, they will guide adult hands and manipulate them to obtain a desired item. This is not a conventional means of communication: the child is not communicating his desire through a common system, but is using the adult hands as objects, in the way that an adult might use a stick to reach a ball that is stuck in a tree.

Developmental patterns differ widely among children with autism. Apart from exhibiting a slower rate of language development, autistic children tend to have a difficult time using the language they learn creatively. Often, they will repeat words and sentences that they hear or use a sentence they were taught in a robot-like manner.

Some children may acquire nouns (i.e. words that map onto concrete objects) easily, yet find it difficult to understand abstract or relational meanings. Still other children may have words and sentences, but lack the ability to use them spontaneously to create a meaningful conversation. When the autistic child's utterances do grow in length, they tend to include a narrower range of grammatical structures. Even in their spontaneous speech, children with autism tend to rely on already learned sentence structures.

Autistic speakers will request objects and actions and utter protests with greater frequency and will display a low frequency of exclamatory statements, reactive statements, and non-focused acts. They can, however, learn to use language and/or other communication skills in a proper and meaningful manner.

Receptive language

Receptive language is the art of understanding. Before one can communicate expressively, one must first have the ability to understand other individuals' signs of communication. Here are a number of receptive language skills that help autistic children to learn the meaning of various communications and focus in on speech and its communicative function:

Pointing/requesting

Pointing is observed in children very early on in their development, and is one of the easiest communication skills to teach.

1. First, find an edible or any item that the child desires. Instead of handing it to him, hold it a bit out of his reach and say 'What do you want?' or 'Point to what you want.'

2. Prompt the child physically to extend his arm toward the item, so as to point with his finger. (Be sure to prompt the use of the right hand for a right-handed child and the left hand for a left-handed child. Whether a child is right-handed or left-handed can be determined by observing which hand he or she normally uses when reaching.)

3. After the child points, give him the item that he pointed to as a reinforcer.

Pointing and requesting can be shaped slowly so that the child does not become frustrated. *For example*: Jenna wants a pretzel.

1. Hold the pretzel a bit out of Jenna's reach, and prompt her to point as described above. Reinforce this prompted response. Practice this step for a number of trials.

2. Hold the pretzel a bit out of Jenna's reach and wait for her to lift her arm towards it. Help her better to point, and then reinforce. Practice this step for a number of trials.

3. Hold the pretzel a bit out of Jenna's reach and only reinforce a perfectly formed point.

4. Work on pointing with other desired items and favorite foods.

5. From now on, Jenna should be expected to point properly for any item which she desires.

Pointing and requesting should be practiced throughout the day, whenever it is clear that the child desires a specific edible or item. Varying the edibles and items that the child requests also helps her to generalize this skill.

Eye contact

Eye contact is important for at least two reasons. It increases awareness and facilitates learning; and it is socially accepted as a part of verbal communication, and so is an important component of integrating a child into the community.

One way to teach eye contact is actually to say, 'Look at me,' and hold a candy, etc., at eye level to prompt the child to look. It is crucial to fade this prompt as quickly as possible, and move toward socially reinforcing the child for looking with a song, tickles, and enthusiastic praise, for this is how eye contact can be maintained in a more natural setting.

Social contacts provide wonderful opportunities to guide a child to look: increase eye contact by waiting for a child to look before engaging him in a preferred activity. *For example:* before each round of Ring-around-the-rosy, Jenna is prompted to look up at her mother in anticipation.

Eye contact will occur spontaneously, if not intentionally, throughout the day. Whenever eye contact is observed, cheer the child on and let him know that he is being wonderfully appropriate. This consistent reinforcement should also help to increase this skill, as well as all attempts at social contact.

Responding-to-name

Recognizing one's own name is a major step in understanding communication. A name connects a sound with an act of attending not simply to an object but to another human being. Call the child's name throughout the day and prompt him to look as a response, either by shading his eyes with your hands, creating tunnel vision, or holding up an edible. Consistency is the key to ensuring that a child makes the connection between hearing his own name and turning his head in recognition. Again, slowly fade the prompt. When a child does respond to his name, make this ritual functional by engaging him in an activity.

It will be more difficult for the child to respond if he is busily engaged in an activity of his own when he is called. Therefore, it may be helpful at first to disengage him from this activity and remove all distractors before calling his name:

1. Sit in front of Jimmy. Make sure that he is not distracted by an alternate activity. Call 'Jimmy' and teach him to respond as illustrated above.

2. Sit a few feet away from Jimmy. Make sure that he is not distracted by an alternate activity. Call 'Jimmy' and teach him to respond.

3. Call Jimmy's name and teach him to respond when he is distracted.

4. Teach Jimmy to respond to his name when he is facing in the opposite direction from you.

5. Call Jimmy from another room, prompt him to come to you and respond with eye contact.

Once a child is working on expressive language, the response 'What?' can be added to his repertoire. Again, it is important to remember not to call the child's name unless you are ready to follow through and prompt/reinforce the correct response. Otherwise, no learning will occur and, in essence, the child's name will lose its meaning as an Sd.

Nouns

Children tend to learn nouns before any other form of speech. Receptive nouns need not be taught only in a discrete trial format. Select a few items that the child comes into contact with often and likes, such as a ball, juice, a toy car and a cookie. Label these items repeatedly, especially after the child points to the item as a request. Remember not to add complicated conversation to the label. Simply say 'ball' when the child is playing with/pointing to the ball, etc.

One-step instructions

Also called commands, one-step instructions are the first communication tool that is taught to the child not for the sole purpose of helping him to attain an item of desire. One-step instructions help caregivers guide a child through daily activities and schedules, and by doing so promote learning. One-step instructions to practice and reinforce in the home include:

- Sit down.
- Wave (a prerequisite for greetings).
- Touch head, nose, mouth, etc.
- Stand up.
- Come here.
- Arms up (helpful for dressing and when a young child needs to be lifted).
- Clap (can be used to redirect hand-flapping and other self-stimulatory behaviors).

Remember to repeat these and other one-step instructions through-out the day in various locations in order to promote generalization, and always reinforce. Also, inform all family members and friends of the instructions that the child is able to follow, so that they can practice these instructions with the child as well.

Two-step instructions

Two-step instructions take one-step instructions further, bringing the child to a higher level of cognitive functioning. Two-step instruc-tions should always be selected building on a child's previous knowledge. Here are some examples of two-step instructions that build on the instructions from the previous example:

- Sit down and touch mouth.
- Stand up and come here.
- Stand up and wave.
- Come here and clap.

Functional instructions and increasing environmental awareness

All instructions can and should be selected for their functional qualities within a home environment. The instruction 'Sit down and touch mouth' is easily prompted and is therefore a good two-step instruction for a child who is first learning this concept. It does not, however, serve a functional purpose. Most often, the instructions which parents find to be the most functional within the home are ones in which the child is told to go to an area of the house ('Go to the bathroom,' 'Go to the livingroom,' 'Go to the table') and ones in which she is told to retrieve an object ('Go get your shoes,' 'Go get your coat,' 'Go get a fork').

These functional instructions also serve the purpose of increasing the child's environmental awareness. They can even be combined into two-step instructions that require even more concentration and understanding, for example: 'Go to the kitchen and get juice,' versus 'Go to the dining-room table and get juice.'

Making a game out of learning language

Language and communication skills, like any other skill, are more easily acquired when learning is fun. Teaching the word 'up' and lifting a child to swing him like an airplane is a common parent–child interaction. Another idea for making language more exciting:

To teach prepositions, instead of using objects, have the child stand 'next to,' 'between,' 'behind,' 'on,' 'under,' and 'in front of' various objects in the house. This requires a lot of movement on the part of the child, and is also a constructive way for her to release energy.

All parents naturally comment on the activities and surroundings of their children, and in doing so expose their children to their first and most valuable verbal stimulation. In order to ensure that this language is meaningful, one must speak to one's child in the child's language-age. A child with autism is not necessarily processing words as easily. Speaking to the child in simple words and shorter sentences and eliminating unnecessary words such as articles ('a', 'the') altogether will reduce the complexity of the communication, and help the child to focus on and learn the words that are crucial to the sentence's meaning. Compare the child to a foreigner learning a second language. The words that are most often repeated in a clear fashion and in the presence of objects or specific activities are the ones that the foreigner will learn first. Only then can these words become the building blocks for understanding more complicated sentences.

Exaggerating one's intonation and the volume at which one speaks when addressing the child will also serve as a prompt and aid to language acquisition. Exaggerated tones capture attention, and let a child know that he is now to tune in to what is being said. Furthermore, the greater the audible difference between various words, the easier it is to differentiate between them. *For example:* Linda had a difficult time discriminating between the words 'livingroom' and 'bedroom.' To help Linda, her mother was told to exaggerate the word 'living' by dragging it out (liiiiiving) and to emphasize the word 'bed' by saying it in a higher pitch.

Although this technique is useful in the initial teaching of language, it must be faded as quickly as possible. Otherwise, the child may begin to tune in to the tone of speech, and not learn to hear the words themselves.

Expressive language

Promoting sounds and babble

Although children with autism often engage in verbal self-stimulation, when a child is first learning to speak and has not yet acquired meaningful words, babbling should be encouraged. Through babble, children explore sounds and sound combinations that are the building blocks of speech. Such verbal exploration can help to develop oral muscles that the child will need as he grows. Furthermore, some children who have difficulty with pronunciation will learn to connect a sound to an item, saying, for example, 'Baaa' for bottle. This labeling is the first step in attaining meaningful speech. Parents who wish to help their child develop expressive language should reinforce and encourage spontaneous utterances, and even babble along with their child.

If a parent is able to distinguish between sound exploration and self-stimulatory babble, self-stimulations should not be reinforced. One way to tell the difference is by listening for repeating sounds. If a child is perseverating on one particular sound to the exclusion of others, he must be encouraged to vary his utterances in order for learning to take place.

Oral motor exercises

Oral motor exercises work on developing the muscles of the mouth and the muscle control that is needed for speech. Oral movements that a child should be able to imitate include:

- opening mouth
- puckering lips
- sticking out tongue

- ○ moving tongue from side to side

- ○ smiling

- ○ chewing

- ○ blowing.

All of these movements can be taught using the discrete trial method, described in Chapter Two. In the discrete trial format, a child not only develops the necessary muscles, but also learns to produce these movements as imitations. Being able to imitate oral movements will help the child, when the time comes, to reproduce sounds and words that he is taught by developing the necessary muscles and training him to attend to the speaker's mouth and carefully observe the oral movements that he must imitate in order to reproduce a sound that he hears.

Verbal imitation

Once a child is able to imitate oral motor movements, he is tuned in to the slight variations of the mouth and tongue that produce various sounds, and is ready to work on verbal imitation. Although some children already speak a number of words or word combinations, verbal imitation can help pronunciation. It is also beneficial for teaching a child to string words together to form sentences.

When working on verbal imitation, it is advisable to begin with imitating simple, one-syllable sounds, move on to sound combinations, and only then teach words. Although this progression is less functional than beginning with word imitation, it follows the speech progression of a child's natural development. Skipping a stage of development could have later repercussions. A child, for example, who learns sound combinations first, may have difficulty isolating a single sound from a combination he learned. To illustrate: Daniel learned to say the word 'banana.' Two weeks later, when he was working on learning his body parts, his mother tried to teach him to say the word 'back.' Every time she prompted him to say 'back,' however, Daniel said 'banana.' He had never learned the sound 'ba-'

as a separate entity, and therefore, when he heard the sound 'ba-', he associated it with the word 'banana' and felt compelled to complete the word.

Verbal imitation clearly affects more than pronunciation. It can help a child to learn sounds, sound combinations and words, and can give him an ability to string word combinations and sentences. Since so much is involved in verbal imitation skills, it is advisable to keep the demands on a child as limited as possible. By shaping responses slowly, reinforcing first approximations and only then perfect responses, one can work within the child's level of frustration and promote greater success.

Requesting

Teaching a child to request expressively is very similar to teaching him to request within a receptive, pointing program. It is, as already mentioned, one of the easiest communication skills to teach. In order to teach a child to request verbally, find an edible or any item that he desires. Rather than simply giving the item to him, hold the item a bit out of his reach, and verbally prompt him to request it.

Jarred wants to eat a pretzel:

1. Hold the pretzel away from Jarred, in his line of vision, and prompt with 'Say "pretzel".' When Jarred says 'pretzel,' give it to him.

2. Hold the pretzel out of Jarred's reach, and only reinforce him with it when he labels it independently, without the prompt.

3. Prompt Jarred to request by saying 'Say, "want pretzel".'

4. Reinforce Jarred with the pretzel only when he requests using the words 'Want pretzel.'

5. Begin working on 'I want pretzel.'

6. Teach Jarred to say, 'I want a pretzel, please.'

It is important to make sure that each of the above steps is mastered before moving on to the next one. In order for a step to be considered mastered, Jarred must be able to respond correctly throughout the day, in various locations, and by communicating with a variety of people whenever possible. It is also important to remember to teach a child to label many different items. Jarred, for example, should not be working on requesting a pretzel to the exclusion of other items and edibles that he desires. If he likes cookies, milk and dolls, step one should include the labeling of all three items throughout the day, etc.

Nouns and object labels

For guidance on teaching nouns, see the advice given in the section on receptive language and commenting to a child in simple language. Object labels can also be taught by asking/responding. Asking a child 'What is it?' when encountering various objects around the house and community, and prompting and reinforcing correct responses, will teach him to label many objects. Beware, however, of using this technique too often, as it also stifles spontaneous speech.

Greetings

Greetings are not only verbal skills, but also social interactions that can vastly increase a child's awareness of his family and peers and help his integration into the community. Take the opportunity to teach greetings whenever anyone, including the child, enters or exits a room. First, work with the child on responding to greetings, then on initiating them. At first, it may be necessary to prompt a child physically by disengaging him from an activity and placing your hand at his wrist to induce a waving motion. It will also be necessary to prompt the child verbally to say 'Hi' or 'Bye bye' and, if possible, the name of the individual the child is greeting. In the case of greetings, modeling and gestural prompts for waving are beneficial in that they will occur in the natural environment. When the child is greeted by a friend, the friend will usually wave, as well. Waving, then, is an appropriate prompt that need not be faded.

Incidental ways of increasing spontaneous language

All children encounter situations that call for the use of speech. By intentionally setting up such situations, one can manipulate the environment to produce requests and proclamations:

Table 6.1	
Situation	*Utterance*
A toy is dropped on the floor/water is spilled.	Uh-oh!/It fell/spilled!
A preferred item is in a zip-lock bag/ container.	Open.
A puzzle is too difficult./The faucet is shut too tightly.	Help me.
The cereal/blocks are on the top shelf.	I want/can you get?
Dinner consists of a small serving.	More please.
The cookie jar is empty.	All gone!
A child wants to be lifted.	Up/pick me up.
During rough play.	Tickles/ tickle me.
A pencil needs sharpening./The light bulb blew.	What should I do?

Select an appropriate situation or two and create the situations a number of times a day for a couple of weeks. Prompt the child to comment appropriately to the situation by saying 'Say "uh-oh",' etc., or simply model the appropriate comment. Always reinforce the child for speaking independently. Once appropriate commenting for these selected situations is consistent, select new ones, and practice them as well.

Social questions

All behaviorally oriented schools for children with autism include a program, for children who have mastered the prerequisite skills, that teaches correct responding to social questions. This program can easily be practiced at home, as well, facilitating generalization. When interacting with your child, ask him questions he has learned in school. If there are additional social questions that you would like your child to be able to answer, work on them, as well, and let the teacher know that you wish them to be taught in class. Important social questions include:

- What is your name?
- Where do you live?
- What is your address?
- What is your phone number?
- How old are you?
- When is your birthday?
- Where do you go to school?
- What is your favorite food?
- Who is in your family?

Other social questions popular among parents are:

- Who is your mommy?
- Who is your daddy?
- Who is your sister/brother?
- Who loves you?
- Who is a good boy/girl?

'Wh-' questions

Note that the preceding section of popular social questions consists entirely of 'who' questions. It is also important for a child to practice the other 'wh-' questions, namely: 'what?' 'when?' 'where?' 'why?' (and 'how?'). Try asking the child two or more different types of 'wh-' questions in the same conversation, and see if she is able to differentiate between them.

Simple formulas

Although the ideal is that the child speak spontaneously using a variety of word and sentence combinations and appropriately varying his inflection, children with autism tend to catch on to formulas and systematically taught speech much more easily. Teaching speech systematically, however, does not detract from a child's ability to learn to speak in a spontaneous voice. In fact, teaching simple formulas enables children to use their verbal skills more frequently and appropriately, in response to situations that arise.

Some examples of simple formulas that will expand a child's verbal repertoire:

- 'Look at what I did! I...'

- 'It is time for...'

Here is how Linda learned to incorporate the first example into her everyday vocabulary:

Linda and her mother were playing with play doh. Linda's mother modeled: 'Look what I did! I made a snake!' Next, they ate lunch. Linda's mother modeled: 'Look what I did! I finished all the crackers!' After a few weeks of modeling these statements, Linda not only learned to say them at appropriate times, but also began to vary the ending based on the situation. One day, Linda said: 'Look what I did! I drew a flower!' With time, Linda learned new formulas that her mother repeatedly modeled for her. Eventually, she even began to expand on the formulas she learned, as well. For instance: 'Look, mommy, I did! I set the table.'

It is clear that teaching formulas does not stifle spontaneity. Rather, it gives the child a linguistic tool that he can apply to a variety of situations and expand upon as necessary. In order to discover new formulas to incorporate into your daily routine, observe other children at play and listen to the speech they naturally use. This will ensure that the formulas taught to the child at home are age appropriate, and will facilitate the child's integration.

Echolalia

Echolalia is imitation of speech. All children progress through a 'parrot' stage at some point in their linguistic development. Children with autism tend to do so at an extreme, and may need help in turning the 'parroting' into functional speech. There are three types of echolalia:

IMMEDIATE ECHOLALIA

This is when a word or sentence is repeated immediately after it is heard. Immediate echolalia can be stopped by teaching a child to say something else, rather than repeating and 'parroting.' *For example*: Daddy says, 'Hi, Samuel.' Samuel replies, 'Hi, Samuel.' To teach Samuel not to echolate but to respond appropriately to the greeting, Daddy says, 'Hi, Samuel,' and after Samuel replies, 'Hi,' but before he has the chance to echolate his own name, his father prompts him to say 'Daddy': 'Hi, Samuel.' 'Hi (say Daddy), Daddy.' This prompt is then faded.

DELAYED, NON-FUNCTIONAL ECHOLALIA

This is when a word or sentence is repeated some time after it is heard. In this case, the child is expressing language but not comprehending it. The language serves the function of a verbal self-stimulation, and is often expressed in the form of routines, such as repeating an entire television segment word for word, often in the same voice and with the same inflection as the actor.

Since delayed, non-functional echolalia provides sensory stimulation, it is the most difficult type of echolalia to reduce. Suggestions for its reduction include stopping the behavior and redirecting the child toward incompatible vocalizations. Ask the child a question. Answering and completing the routine are incompatible, and the routine should end. Also, do not allow the child to engage in reinforcing activities while he is echolating. Take away his puzzle and tell him that he needs to work quietly. As soon as he is quiet, allow him to continue to work on the puzzle.

DELAYED, FUNCTIONAL ECHOLALIA

This is when a language statement is taken as a whole and over-generalized to other situations. *For example*: in the morning, when Tara threw her toy and broke a vase, her mother said, 'Look what you did, now go to your room.' At lunchtime, Tara accidentally spilled her juice and echolated, 'Look what you did, now go to your room.' Tara is 'parroting' a sentence that she heard earlier in the day, but she is also using the sentence functionally (almost appropriately, but over-generalized).

Children with autism who use delayed echolalia functionally may be on their way to learning language and its appropriate use. To help a child speak more functionally, try to prompt her to say a sentence that is similar to the one echolated, yet more appropriate to the situation and expressed in different, non-'parroting' words. *For example*: prompt Tara to say, ' Look what I did, now I clean it up.'

Reciprocal conversation

Reciprocal conversations consist of more than questions and answers. A number of reciprocal conversations one can practice at home are as follows:

1. **While playing**

    Statement: 'I am playing with a doll.'

    Child's response: 'I am playing with Lego.'

2. **While looking at a book or out the window**

    Statement: 'I see a red flower.'

    Child's response: 'I see a tree.'

3. **While looking in a mirror**

    Statement: 'My hair is brown.'

    Child's response: 'My hair is brown, too.'

4. **With peers**

    Statement: 'I have a dog.'

    Child's response: 'I have a cat.'

    Statement: 'My dog's name is Henry.'

    Child's response: 'My cat's name is Cinnamon.'

Practicing a variety of reciprocal conversations with a child will prepare the child for social encounters with family and friends.

Modeling and expansion

Modeling and expansion is very similar to the way in which formulas are taught. A parent or peer models a sentence at its appropriate time, repeating it throughout the day for a number of weeks or until the child learns to use the sentence. In this case, however, the parent does not wait for the child to vary the sentence and add to it. Instead, systematic expansion is modeled, as well. *For example*: Samuel's mother models the sentence: 'I see a car.' Once Samuel learns to say, 'I see a car' when he sees one, Samuel's mother models the sentence, 'I see a blue car.' She teaches Samuel to say 'Mommy, I see a blue car next to the tree,' etc.

Pronouns

Children with autism usually have difficulty using correct pronouns. This difficulty could stem from echolalia (a child hears, 'Do you want more soup?' and then requests by saying, 'You want more soup.'). To help her learn how to use pronouns correctly, practice using pronouns with her.

1. Begin by asking the child: 'Touch my nose/tummy/knee' v. 'Touch your nose/tummy/knee.' Body parts are a part of the individual and are easier to learn than possessions.

2. Next, ask the child: 'Touch my shirt/hat/watch' v. 'Touch your shirt/hat/watch,' – items that are somehow connected to the individual.

3. Select an item. Take one for yourself and give one to the child. Then ask the child: 'Touch my pencil/block/cup' v. 'Touch your pencil/block/cup.'

4. Start from the beginning, and work on 'his' v. 'her', 'their' v. 'our.'

Practice conversation

It is very important for children with advanced conversational skills to practice conversing so that they can smooth any residual linguistic errors. Practicing conversation with an aware adult will enable the child to work on varying the wording of his initiations, varying responses, and using proper intonation. Some children have difficulty speaking at proper volume, as well. For them, it is also helpful to practice saying specific words and phrases alternating between a loud and a soft voice.

Sometimes children who are unable to express themselves through language will resort to other, unconventional means of communication such as tantruming and aggression. Practicing conventional means of expressing feelings such as hunger and anger will give a child an alternative outlet for these maladaptive behaviors.

Furthermore, children who find self-expression difficult may often get frustrated. To reduce this frustration, teach a child to relay to others that he is having difficulty. Work on conversational phrases such as: 'This is hard,' and 'I don't know.'

Scripts

Introducing scripts during an activity, for literate children, is a good way of forming a discussion without having to prompt a child verbally throughout the conversation. Scripts can include directions and dialogue. Just as with simple formulas, children who practice written scripts gain a language tool that they are then able to use in many situations and with personal, spontaneous variations. An example of a script is as follows:

(*Sally –*)

Go get the tea set.

Walk up to Linda and ask her: 'Wanna play with me?'

(*Linda –*)

Look at Sally and say: 'OK, I'll be the mommy.'

(*Sally and Linda –*)

Set the table and sit down.

(*Linda –*)

Ask Sally: 'Would you like some tea?'

(*Sally –*)

Look at Linda and say: 'I want tea with milk and sugar.'

(*Linda –*)

Pour tea for Sally. Add milk. Add sugar.

(*Sally –*)

Go to the kitchen set. Open the oven. Say: 'I think the muffins are ready.' Bring the muffins to the table. Take a muffin and give one to Linda.

(*Sally and Linda –*)

Pretend to eat the muffins and drink the tea.

(*Linda –*)

Say: 'These are delicious!'

Scripts can be written for practically any activity. Again, it is important to observe children at play before authoring a script, in order to ensure that the script is geared toward the child and his peers, and that it includes the words and the slang that are popular within the child's age group. Before giving a script to two or more children, practice the script with each child in a one-on-one setting, with you acting as the other child/ren in the script. Once the script is mastered with an adult, it is easier to practice with a peer. Eventually, the written script can be faded from the activity and the children playing should independently add sentences and vary the script accordingly.

Sign language

Sign language is a conventional means of communication used throughout society by individuals of varying developmental disabilities. Sign language may be beneficial to children with autism if the following indications are observed:

1. The child, after lengthy behavioral training and speech therapy, exhibits little or no vocalization.

2. The child tends to understand gestures easily, and quickly learns to point in order to request items of desire.

3. The child's receptive language skills surpass his expressive language skills, and his inability to communicate thoughts and feelings often leaves him frustrated.

If a sign language program is indeed decided upon, the following signs are easy to teach and will help to ease frustration at the beginning of this new program:

> more
> food
> drink
> bathroom
> I want
> music
> nod head: yes
> shake head: no.

Communication boards

Since children with autism usually have difficulty understanding gestures, another conventional means of communication was created for them: communication boards allow their users to communicate without the use of voice and without the need for gestures or signs.

Three-dimensional communication boards

Three-dimensional communication boards consist of small, three-dimensional models of objects that the child may desire. To create this type of communication board, select items the child needs and likes, find them in shops and/or catalogs (see Chapter Nine), and velcro them onto a cardboard sheet so that they are easily removable by the child. Practice using the communication board, as follows: hold up an item and physically prompt the child to remove the small model representing that item from the cardboard sheet. Prompt the child to give you the model in exchange for the actual item.

Picture exchange systems

A picture exchange system incorporates pictures as a means of communication in the same way that the board described above uses three-dimensional miniature models. Some recommend using picture exchange systems along with a verbal program in order to facilitate and speed up the language-learning process. One popular picture exchange system on the market is 'Boardmaker' (by Mayer-Johnson). With this system, even complicated word combinations are represented. Simpler picture exchange systems can also be created by cutting pictures from magazines. If a child has difficulty with representations, try taking snapshots of the actual items the child will request. Photograph all of the items against the same solid background to minimize distraction and confusion.

If a communication board is created for a child, it must be available to him at all times. Practical communication boards are small in size and easily carried. Remember that the purpose of the communication board is to allow the child to communicate, and with use, practice, and exposure, spontaneous communications will increase in frequency. For literate children, computer writing pads can be explored as an option, as well.

Conclusion

Teaching a child to communicate meaningfully will increase his ability to interact socially, and reduce his frustration, resulting in fewer maladaptive behaviors.

Receptive language skills to teach include:

- pointing/requesting

- eye contact

- responding-to-name

- nouns

- one-step instructions

- two-step instructions

- functional instructions.

Functional instructions and nouns will help to increase a child's environmental awareness. A child who is aware of his surroundings is more likely to learn language. Making a game out of language (such as teaching a child to say 'up' before lifting him to swing him like an airplane, and other examples given in this chapter) will also increase language acquisition by making learning fun.

Expressive language skills to teach include:

- appropriate sounds and babble

- oral motor exercises

- verbal imitation

- requesting

- nouns and object labels

- greetings

- ° social questions

- ° simple formulas

- ° reciprocal conversation

- ° pronouns

- ° scripts.

Practicing conversations will ensure maintenance and generalization and will help an advanced conversationalist to learn how to vary his responses appropriately. Alternative communication methods include sign language and picture exchange systems. These means of communication are considered to be conventional and are easily adapted into the community.

CHAPTER 7

Sibling Interaction

Introduction: The importance of establishing a positive sibling relationship early on

Positive sibling relationships among children not only make day-to-day living within a family more pleasant, but also create a life-long support system for the siblings involved. A relationship of love and support can be both more difficult to establish and more crucial in a family where one of the siblings copes daily with a developmental disorder.

Siblings of children with autism may face the following challenges:

1. It may be difficult for a sibling to understand the nature of autism and why his or her brother or sister exhibits certain behaviors. Furthermore, some behaviors, such as aggression and self-stimulation, may be scarier when observed at eye-level.

2. Siblings may feel that they are not receiving as much attention as the child with autism. Often, in-home therapy programs are conducted in a room which siblings are forbidden to enter. During therapy, they may hear the child with autism being praised repeatedly and feel jealousy.

3. Candies may be presented to the child with autism frequently, whereas snacks may not be as easily accessible to siblings.

4. Older siblings may face a loss of attention that they received prior to their younger sibling's diagnosis. They may fall into a role of support for the mother and experience her grief.

5. Younger siblings may find that their role is reversed, and that they are expected to care for their older, autistic sibling. They may find themselves with responsibilities greater than those of other children of their age.

6. Often, siblings face teasing from their peers. As children, they may not have the emotional or verbal knowledge and tools with which to combat this feeling of ridicule, nor may they understand that they are not alone in this situation.

All of these challenges and numerous others can affect the way a sibling forms familial relationships, peer relationships, and even his or her own concept of self. Before a parent can begin to work on establishing a positive sibling relationship, it is important that the parent understand the sibling involved. In order to do so, one must realize that not only the behavior of the child with autism, but also the behavior of a sibling is somewhat shaped by his or her environment. Behaviors are usually motivated by a variety of intricate goals and feelings, some conscious and some subconscious. A parent's reaction to the sibling can help to guide the sibling toward strong coping skills, love and understanding for the child with autism, and love and positive feelings for his or her self.

It is also important for a parent to realize early on that a child with a disability may come to rely on his or her sibling increasingly as they both mature, even in areas such as guardianship and support, and prepare for this possibility. In adulthood, a sibling who feels equality and attachment will view this situation not as a burden but as a serious and wanted responsibility. Love between siblings must be established at a young age in order for the positive relationship to last for a lifetime.

Teaching siblings about autism

Discussing autism with one's child can be difficult and can raise many questions with which parents may struggle both on a practical and on an emotional level. Neither parents nor professionals have all of the answers, but it is important for parents to realize that children usually have none of the answers, and when this is the case they tend to create their own ideas of why the child with autism behaves as he does. These misconceptions can be very damaging. Examples of misconceptions may include:

> My brother doesn't play with me because he doesn't like me.

> My brother is sick and may die.

> My sister has an autism that I can catch.

> My parents give my sister so much attention because they love her more than they love me.

Although it may be difficult at first, approaching the topic of autism with the other children in the family will prove to be very fruitful. It will help to dissolve any harmful misconceptions, provide knowledge and a language a child needs in order to be able to cope with his feelings toward situations that may arise in the family or with peers, and allow the child to have a better understanding of the behaviors that the sibling with autism may exhibit. This understanding can only lead in the direction of love rather than confusion and possible fear.

When discussing autism with children, explanations should be as short and simple as possible. Speak to children on a level that they will understand. On the other hand, be careful not to underestimate their understanding and curiosity. Do, however, make sure to answer their questions using words that they will be able to repeat if they are asked about their sibling.

Take children and their concerns seriously. Make sure that they are comfortable asking questions, and let them know that you do not have all the answers. Honest answers are complete answers.

Reassure them that both they and the child with autism are safe and loved. This can be accomplished by saying 'I love you' to each child in the presence of the other. Furthermore, tell children verbally that autism is not fatal, nor is it contagious. Showing love is always important, but in this case they may need to be told explicitly that they do not have to worry about their safety, etc. Ask them if they have any other concerns, and address those directly as well.

Although it is important to respond to a child's inquiries, do not allow him to obsess on the topic of autism. It is not healthy for you or for the child, and is often a sign that he is seeking undivided parental attention that can be provided in other ways. If the child has no questions or concerns, do not force the topic.

Let the child know that there are other children in his situation. Speak to other parents and set up play dates for the siblings of children with autism. Children, as well as adults, need peer support. Bringing siblings to the school so that they can observe their brother or sister with autism learning with other children will also serve as a form of support. It will provide them with an opportunity to talk to the teachers and see that there are other children like their brother or sister. The trip will make them feel important and included, and that feeling, in and of itself, will have a positive effect on the sibling relationship.

Finally, prepare children for difficult situations with peers and in the community. Sharing some of your own experiences with a child who has encountered teasing from his peers will help him to put the teasing into perspective:

- It will let him know and feel that he is not alone.

- It will help him to understand that people often make fun of others out of ignorance.

- It will help him to realize that what other people think is not always important.

- It will help him decide how to respond to the jeering.

- It will give him a more optimistic view with regard to the situation.

Practice with the child statements that she may use in difficult situations in response to questions and possible ridicule from her friends. In doing so, however, make sure that the statements selected are statements children would make to each other. For example:

A child who responds to ridicule with a statement such as: ' I love my brother and am proud of him, even on difficult days,' or 'My sister has autism,' most likely does not understand his own responses. A child's response must serve to help him understand his own feelings with regard to the situation, as well as serving to end the feeling of ridicule. Teach a child that yes, his brother or sister with autism may act weird at times, but he or she is also a great sibling. Teach him to say things like: 'My brother may not be good at talking, but he can do almost any puzzle in the world,' 'Yeah, she acts weird sometimes,' or 'He doesn't like waiting. Did you ever see how fast he can run?'

Encourage the child to come up with her own statements about her sibling with autism. Review with the child her own strengths and weaknesses. Perhaps she is great at math, but needs some help in spelling. Drawing this parallel makes autism and therapy easier to understand.

Creating a sense of equality

All children are different and equality is not a realistic standard. Nevertheless, children need to feel equal to their siblings in the eyes of their parents. The exercise described above teaches the child that both she and her sibling with autism have strengths and weaknesses. They both need to work on their weaknesses a bit harder and they both enjoy certain activities more than others. Seeing these similarities helps to create a sense of equality and camaraderie among siblings.

A child who has a sibling with autism may not easily recognize the pride that her parents feel with regard to her own achievements. Since the child with autism is praised continuously for even small successes, it may be necessary to pay extra attention to his siblings' successes, and perhaps reward and reinforce the siblings' positive behavior frequently as well.

Siblings of a child with autism may benefit from a reward system based on homework completion or good grades in a difficult subject. Chores around the house can be instituted as the child with autism is learning functional tasks, so that the siblings can work alongside each other. For example, if the child with autism is working on setting the table, a sibling may be asked to wash the dishes or take out the garbage, and then they can be rewarded with a snack together (sharing a snack is a positive activity that siblings can share and that is naturally reinforcing).

If therapy sessions are conducted in the children's room and during therapy the sibling is excluded from that area, create a special private time during which the sibling can also be alone in the room.

The sibling as a child and as an individual

A child with a developmental disorder will naturally need more attention and take up more of parents' time than one who needs less help in daily activities. Spending quality time with the other children in the family, however, does not necessarily mean taking time away from the child with autism. Quality time is time during which the child is the priority. Parents who set aside even ten minutes a day to give their full attention to each child as an individual will find that resentment toward the sibling with the disability quickly decreases.

When spending quality time with your child, be sure to engage in an activity that she enjoys. Whenever possible, let her select the activity. That will further her feeling that you are there for her and that it is her special time.

Conversation is a wonderful activity that can take almost no time at all. Ask the child about his day at school, about a project he did or a ball game in which he participated, and listen to him without interruption. Do not use this time to discuss autism.

Sometimes it is to easy to use a child as a sounding board, but it is important to remember that children need to be children and should not be their parents' support system. In conversation, it is also important to be careful not to project your own feelings and needs onto the child.

If the sibling is taking on responsibilities beyond his or her age-level, his own childhood and development will suffer. Of course his help will be needed. Whenever possible, however, try not to rely on his help. Siblings of a child with autism should not feel that the work and responsibilities they share are a burden. Additionally, it is natural to have high expectations for the siblings of a child with a disability. Nevertheless, it is natural for them to make mistakes as well, especially ones that are attention-seeking. Remember that a sibling is not just a sibling. He is a child with all of the needs and cares of a child.

Creating a positive sibling relationship

Teaching your children about autism, making them feel equally important and, in some ways, similar to their sibling (perhaps they both like cereal/books/Elmo) and providing them with personal quality time will serve as the building blocks for creating a positive sibling relationship. Here are some other ideas for promoting positive sibling interaction:

1. **Instead of thinking of all the things the children do not yet do together that you would like to encourage, begin by making a list of the activities that they do share**. If the children watch television together, make that a special time. Introduce the activity by saying, 'Come watch TV with your sister/brother,' and let the children know how nice it is that they are enjoying the show together. This will provide positive reinforcement for the child with autism and help the other children to feel that they are sharing positive time with their sibling.

2. **Encourage them to play side by side**. If the child with autism likes to play with dinosaurs and his sister likes to play with blocks, they can do so at the same time and in the same room. Sharing space is in and of itself beneficial to a relationship, even without interaction.

3. **Teach siblings some simple rules of applied behavior analysis (ABA)**. Once you are ready to increase interaction among siblings during game-playing, it can be very helpful to incorporate some of the tools used by parents and professionals and provide children with knowledge that will help them to get the child with autism to respond. Teach them by using these simple suggestions:

    1. Call your brother's name before talking to him.

    2. Make sure he is looking at you and paying attention.

    3. Give him one instruction at a time.

    4. Count to three in your head and give him time to think of what he is supposed to do.

    5. If you have to ask him again, go over and show him what you want.

    6. Say 'Thank you' and clap and cheer when he is doing it right, because he will learn that way.

Remember to reinforce both children for interacting nicely, especially if a child's efforts are met with little reciprocation from his autistic sibling.

It is amazing how quickly children who are taught these instructions pick them up and work well presenting Sds, prompting and reinforcing without any formal ABA training and without knowing ABA terms. A sibling can be an excellent teacher as well as friend, and can gain the beautiful feeling of guiding another and seeing him learn and grow.

4. **Increase the likelihood that the child with autism will initiate sibling interaction**. Have the sibling hold a toy that the child with autism likes to play with (or even a reinforcing edible). Grabbing should not be allowed: the sibling should wait for the child with autism to initiate before giving him the preferred item.

Initiating by holding a preferred item is beneficial only if the siblings involved are old enough to understand that they must give the toy away once the child with autism has requested it properly. Doing so should help to increase the frequency with which the child with autism approaches her siblings at other times throughout the day. This is because her approaching behavior was systematically reinforced by the sibling giving her the preferred item, which acted as a natural reinforcer.

This exercise should only be done with siblings who are old enough to understand that once the child with autism initiates, the toy has to be shared. Giving her preferred items to hold will increase sibling interaction throughout the day because the child with autism will learn that approaching her sibling can be very reinforcing.

5. **Practice turn-taking games with siblings**. Turn-taking games, unlike many other sibling interactions, require few verbal skills. The game itself acts as a reinforcer, though verbal and edible reinforcers can be provided by the parent throughout the game if necessary (remember to reinforce both children). Use a game that the child with autism has already mastered. When first introducing this game to siblings, you may need to supervise the activity and even prompt the child with autism from behind in order to ensure proper turn-taking.

6. **Have siblings work on gross motor imitation together**. Gross motor activities are fun and easy to prompt. Younger children can imitate together with a parent acting as the leader. Adding the words 'Simon says' in front of each instruction should not alter the autistic child's ability to respond correctly and will make the activity more fun for the other children involved. Older siblings can be the leader, eliminating parental involvement. This activity will allow an older sibling the opportunity to feel successful, in charge, significant and fun in the eyes of the child with autism.

Providing siblings of an autistic child with these guidelines helps the child with autism to learn. More importantly, however, it allows the siblings to be successful in their attempts at interaction, creating a better feeling and a more positive sibling relationship overall.

When not to include siblings

In order for the activities described above and other sibling interactions to be successful, remember that not all sibling interaction is positive. Siblings should be included in an activity only when there is a high likelihood that it will be successful. Otherwise, a sibling may feel that failure is his fault or that the child with autism does not like him. Avoiding a situation that can lead to negative feelings means not including a sibling in an activity when:

- the activity has not been mastered with an adult

- the activity is not enjoyed by even one of the children involved

- the environment may be distracting (i.e. father just came home from work or the television is on)

- the child with autism had to be redirected from a more reinforcing activity such as self-stimulatory behavior or reading a book

- the sibling of the child with autism does not want to play.

Some situations are not always predictable. Even an activity planned for in detail may not always turn out to be positive. Planning for success, however, will increase the likelihood that interactions among siblings are both positive and meaningful. This planning includes being aware of situations that may affect an activity, and working around them as described above.

The positive effects that having a sibling with autism can have on a child

Siblings of children with autism grow up learning the importance of supporting those around them, and of seeking support when they are in need. They also tend to share the following qualities:

- increased patience
- the ability to nurture
- acceptance and tolerance of others
- heightened compassion and empathy.

Siblings of children with autism, like those of children with other disabilities, understand that life is not always fair, and so are able to love and celebrate life and the various directions it takes.

Conclusion

Sibling relationships represent the first peer relationships that we experience. They also represent the longest relationship in our lives. Although this relationship may change over time, it is a permanent one, and one of great emotional significance. The relationship that siblings share is very important to their development as they grow from children to adults, especially when there is the possibility of a greater need for them to care for each other as they mature.

Cultivating a positive sibling relationship can be a challenging task for any parent. Positive sibling relationships are also natural, and children who share their childhood will feel a special connection to each other. In order to help siblings of a child with autism find their place in the family and develop an even stronger sibling relationship, remember to:

- teach siblings about autism
- create a sense of equality among the siblings whenever possible
- increase positive sibling interaction
- relate to siblings not just as siblings, but as individuals.

CHAPTER 8

Bringing a Child with Autism into the Community

Introduction: The importance of generalizing skills and being an active community member

Generalization occurs when a behavior demonstrated in one specific situation is exhibited in other, similar situations as well (see Chapter Two). Generalizing a skill is the only way to ensure that a mastered skill will help a child in all aspects of life. The child will be able to use and exhibit that skill at home, in school, at the playground, in a store, in a restaurant and throughout the community. He will be able to exhibit the skill with all people, and in a variety of situations.

Children who are active community members are exposed to many more learning opportunities than those who spend their time at home. Parents, as well, need to be able to take their children out in order to accomplish many daily chores and in order to become a part of the adult community.

Children with autism do not automatically generalize all of the skills that they learn. Promoting generalization takes work and practice. A child with autism needs to work on all skills in a variety of locations and to practice skills throughout all walks of life. Supervising an autistic child outside of the home can be, at times, a challenge. Outings can also be very positive occasions if they are prepared for properly. Preparation for outings that are positive experiences involve:

- ◦ reviewing destinations and preferred activities

- ◦ preparing the child for entering the community

- ◦ bringing along the necessary materials

- ◦ emotional preparation for the parent.

Parents who are confident with their child, and with their parenting, will be better equipped to handle any situation that may arise.

Reviewing destinations and preferred activities

Reviewing destinations and preferred activities will help to make outings into the community more pleasant for both the child and the parents. Review destinations and preferred activities as follows:

- ◦ Think of activities in which the child can participate, and include them in the outing. Outings are more successful when they include events in which the child can actively participate. Before leaving the house, think of the destination and come up with a few possible activities that the child might enjoy at that destination. For example: at a birthday party, request an interactive song with which the child is familiar.

- ◦ Take the opportunity to practice mastered skills outside the home environment. Many mastered skills can indeed be practiced outside. Structuring a child's time and involving him during the outing will decrease inappropriate behaviors during that time.

- ◦ *in the park/on a walk*: practice the commands 'stop' and 'go.' Work on other verbs such as running, walking, hopping, and jumping

- ◦ *in a department store*: review colors, items of clothing, and self-dressing skills

- ◦ *at the grocery*: teach requesting and choice-making.

- ◦ Involve the child whenever possible. Involving a child can be accomplished by practicing mastered skills such as those suggested above. Other ideas for involving children in outside activities:

- *at the zoo:* involve the child by asking him the names of the animals and the sounds they make

- *during holiday parties:* practice social greetings, play skills, and task completion. Toys such as puzzles, peg boards, and 'Mr. Potato Head' can be brought along.

Outings in which the child is directed and involved will be easier to manage and will be more exciting for the child.

- *Practice the activities involved in difficult outings in small, incremental steps, at home.* Often, a parent must bring a child to a destination where the child is not yet able to participate in the activities and tasks involved. Such destinations include the bank, the post office, a ticket line and more. In this case it is helpful to practice the outing with the child at home, in small steps.

- *Have the family stand in a line and wait patiently for a candy every weekend.* Gradually increase the time that the child must spend waiting on line before he receives the candy. This practice will make standing on line when out in the community less cumbersome, especially if reinforcers are brought along.

- *Walking appropriately can also be practiced.* Take time to bring the child on short walks during the week. First, reinforce the child for walking down the block, then around the corner, etc. This will ease outings for parents who feel that they need to carry their child frequently.

- *Alternate non-preferred activities with activities that the child enjoys.* Schedule activities in the community so that they occur in a reinforcing order. Limit time spent in a non-preferred activity, and then begin a preferred activity. For example: if a child dislikes McDonald's but loves to go to the playground, go to McDonald's for a short meal consisting of two chicken nuggets (or a different food that the child enjoys) and, immediately upon completion of the meal, spend some time in the playground. Eventually, McDonald's will become less aversive, for it will signify a fun activity to follow. Other restaurants can then be introduced in the same fashion.

Alternating non-preferred activities with activities that the child enjoys will make the day seem easier overall. Over time, it will also teach the child to be patient during non-preferred activities.

- Save difficult activities for days in which the child is more relaxed. Whenever possible, save the most difficult outings for days and times when the child is calm and better able to handle stress. Remember that a child with autism is not 'being difficult' but, rather, is expressing a lack of understanding or ability to cope with his environment and feelings of discomfort. Choose your battles. No child can improve in every category at once, and some activities may be too difficult for the child on a particular day or at his current stage of development.

- Save difficult activities for a day that is good for you. Parents need to be prepared to handle difficult behaviors calmly. If a parent has had a hard day at the office, or for any other reason is feeling an overload of stress, that parent's needs must be considered. This is not the time to bring a child to a destination where she is likely to tantrum. Take the child out at a time when you know that you will have the patience to attend to any behaviors that may arise.

Preparing the child for entering the community

Spending time in the home practicing situations and activities that the child will encounter on an outing is the best preparation that she can have for entering the community. Teach her to expect certain situations, and then give her the communication tools that she will need in order to react to new situations that inevitably arise. This will make the process of entering the community much easier, despite any difficulties that the child may encounter along the way. (Carol Gray has developed social stories that can help prepare individuals with autism for a variety of situations: see references, Chapter Nine.)

Provide the child with the schedule of the day ahead of time. All children, as well as adults, work better with the expected than with the unexpected. Children with autism, who have even greater difficulties transitioning from one activity to the next, will find outings much more bearable if there are fewer surprises and the activities for the day are more predictable. There are various ways in which a child can be provided with a schedule:

- Take pictures of the day's activities and attach them to a wall within the child's reach. This way you can review the activities in the morning, and/or before beginning each activity. Using velcro to attach the pictures to the wall will allow the child, whenever possible, to select the order in which he will complete the day's activities.

- Written schedules are useful in reminding a literate child of his daily routine. If the routine has to be changed, writing the change in the schedule will decrease anxiety that may result from unpredictability.

- Children who are good at sequencing can be told of the day's schedule verbally. For example: 'First we are going to the bank. After going to the bank, we will go to the bagel store.' Take an extra minute to make sure that the child understands the order of the activities. Ask the child: 'Where are we going first?' and 'Where are we going after we go to the bank?'

Select a schedule that is appropriate both for the activities and for the child's level of understanding. A child can use more than one type of schedule depending on his needs. *For example:* Ryan has a written schedule for his morning routine. This schedule is attached to his door to remind him to get dressed, go to the bathroom, bring his schoolbag to the front door, and eat breakfast. He also has a schedule consisting of photographs for when he goes out into the community. This schedule is made with velcro. If, on a given day, Ryan is going to the grocery, the library and the pool, he velcros these pictures to a small album and carries them with him as a reminder.

Schedules help a child to transition from activity to activity throughout the day. When scheduling is not possible, giving a child warning that an activity is about to end will help make the transition into the next activity run more smoothly. Some children are ready to use this opportunity to learn how to tell time. For children who are not yet ready for a watch, a signal can be developed by the parent and consistently used to indicate transition time. *For example:* Sally did not want to go to the park. Once she was playing in the sandbox, however, she wanted to stay there, and would not go in the pool. After she was in the pool for a while, she refused to get out of the water for lunch. Sally's mother created a signal for her that indicated transition time. Two minutes before Sally had to leave the house to go to the park, her mother rang a bell. She also rang the bell two minutes before Sally had to come out of the sand box, leave the pool, or end any activity to begin the next. Now Sally is able to prepare herself, and smoother transitioning occurs.

Bells are signals that are commonly used in classrooms to indicate that recess is over and the lesson is about to begin. Other possible signals include a red sign for 'stop' and a green sign for 'go,' songs and flickering of lights. Once a signal is selected, it must be used consistently for all transitions in order to remain effective.

Teaching a child to communicate his wishes will enable him to gain social reinforcement and approval when in the community, and to avoid possible discomfort:

- Teach the child a way to escape an uncomfortable situation. A child who knows how to say 'no' will be less likely to tantrum or cause a commotion when he is expected to engage in an unwanted activity, such as eating a food that he does not like or putting on a sweater when he is hot.

- Teach appropriate ways of bringing an activity to an end. A child should be able to express her wish to leave a situation. Giving her the vocabulary to say 'I don't want to be here,' or 'I don't want to do this,' does not mean that her wish will be granted each time it is requested, but it does open the lines of communication. This way, when it is possible for her to leave a situation or end an activity, she can do so in a proper fashion and be reinforced for requesting it appropriately.

○ Teach social assertiveness. Young children tend to take toys and other items from one another. Teaching a child to tell a friend, 'Give it back,' will reduce the crying that occurs after a toy is taken away and increase a child's assertiveness in any social setting in which he is required to interact with siblings and/or peers.

○ Teach the child how to ask for a break. Sometimes it may be possible to allow a child who wants to leave a situation to do so for a short period of time. Instead of crying and having to be led out by the parent until he is quiet, the child can express the need for escape by saying, 'I need/want a break,' and the parent can take him for a short walk or a drink of water.

○ Teach a child how to ask for more time. Often we take for granted a child's ability to ask for five more minutes in the park or ten more minutes at the pool. It is much more difficult for children with autism to grasp this concept of time. For children with strong communication skills, however, asking for more time to spend engaging in an activity is similar to asking for more food or more blocks, and teaching this concept is a worthwhile effort.

At the very first signs that the child does not wish to end his current activity, prompt him to say so, using the words, 'I'm not ready,' 'Can I stay?' or 'Soon.' Then allow him to engage in the activity for five or ten minutes longer. (Expect a protest after those ten minutes are up, until the child fully learns this concept.)

Giving a child a daily schedule provides him with the predictability that autistic children often need, and can enable the child to participate in the organization of the day's activities. Since schedules cannot provide complete predictability, remember that signaling before transitions can help a child to prepare to move from one activity to another. It is also important to provide him with skills for communicating his reactions and needs as new situations arise, especially if these involve social interaction. Finally, always try to give the child possibilities and allow him to make choices. Often, he will reject both a coloring book and a party blower, but if offered a choice between the two will happily select one. Even allowing a child to carry either the grapes or the bread in a supermarket is giving him the opportunity to make his own choices and become involved in the activity.

Bringing along the necessary materials

Materials from home allow a parent to turn an unsuccessful outing into a successful one. A child who is not engaging in the community activity at which he is present can work on a shape-sorter, string beads, flip through a book or play with a toy car. Instead of being unsuccessful, he can now engage appropriately in tasks that he has mastered, and remain occupied. When selecting items to bring along on an outing, keep in mind the following:

- The items selected should occupy and stimulate the child. Bring along games that he is able to use independently and that take some time to complete. Bring toys that the child enjoys, so that playing with them appropriately is reinforcing.

- Edible reinforcers are easy to carry and easy to give a child when toys are not an option (such as while walking or in a place of prayer). Candies, animal crackers and licorice are examples of edible reinforcers that can be used subtly to reinforce appropriate and quiet behavior in the community.

- For children who engage in self-stimulatory behaviors, it may be necessary to provide alternative sensory input. This could mean bringing along a walkman to provide auditory input for a child who sings out loud, or a kaleidoscope to provide visual input for one who likes to go cross-eyed. Sometimes the material that provides the alternative sensory input is less than appropriate and would not be allowed in the home, but is necessary in order to complete an outing into the community successfully. For example: the benefits of having a string for a child to play with quietly may outweigh its inappropriateness.

○ Bringing a variety of items makes it more likely that one of them will be desired by the child. Remember that a child may want a puzzle one day and a doll the next. Variety also allows her to select her own reinforcer/toy with which to play, increasing independence through choice-making.

Always remember to reinforce a child's appropriate behavior. The key to helping him succeed in a community outing is not just to bring along the necessary materials, but to use those materials at the proper time. Do not give him a reinforcing item when he is tantruming. That will reinforce maladaptive behavior. Rather, reinforce him periodically from the start in order to prevent the tantrum altogether. If he does exhibit inappropriate behavior in public, try to redirect him to behavior that is more appropriate before giving him a reinforcing item.

Emotional preparation for parents

Often parents find that when they are in the community with their child and behaviors surface, people in the vicinity are eager to give advice and comment on the situation. All parents have heard disapproving statements such as, 'This child should have been left with a sitter!' 'Look how they spoil him!' and 'What are they doing to that child!' These exclamations can be very painful to hear, especially for parents of a child with autism.

Autism is not well known or understood by much of society. Its symptoms are not always easily detectable, and a child with autism does not have any physical features that distinguish him from other children. Parents of children with disabilities such as Down's syndrome or cerebral palsy find that the community is sympathetic and understanding toward their children, and can count on the community for support. Parents of children with autism are not necessarily able to benefit from such support, for members of the community are not necessarily able to detect that the child with autism is struggling and in need of special attention and love.

It is natural for any parents who hear a hurtful statement concerning their child to react. Typical reactions can include a sharp, painful response, a lengthy and highly personal explanation, a brief explanation, a lie, and/or silent tears. Depending on the situation, all of these reactions may be appropriate. Emotional preparation for encounters with unsympathetic community members, however, will help to prepare you so that uncomfortable situations are resolved more smoothly. Reactions should not feed discomfort, but rather should be aimed at easing inner tension and increasing your ability to cope and handle your child's behavior properly.

Enter the community knowing that, as a parent, you have knowledge of your child, autism, and professionally accepted behavioral techniques. Although no parent is perfect and all parents are allowed to make some mistakes and encounter some difficulties, you are adept at caring for your child.

Understand also that your response to another community member will probably not give him or her enough insight into the struggle that you and your child with autism face every day. Go out prepared to deal with other community members. Responses that are simple and explanations that state facts are more easily understood. Remember, though, that your response is not for their emotional benefit, but yours.

Following are examples of statements parents may frequently encounter when out in the community. For each statement, four counteracting sentences are given. The first two (Response A) can serve as a mental reaction that you can say to yourself whenever you feel that it would be helpful. The second two (Response B) can be your verbal response to the hurtful comment you have encountered.

1. **Statement**

   'That child should have been left at home with a babysitter!'

Responses

A) 'By taking him out with me, I provide my child with many more learning experiences and opportunities to grow than he would ever have at home with a babysitter.'

A) 'If she/he has children, they experienced difficult days, as well.'

B) 'I cannot teach my child how to behave in public if he is never allowed out of the house.'

B) 'I love my child and am proud of him, even on difficult days.'

2. **Statement**

'Look at how those parents spoil the boy/girl!'

Responses

A) 'If only they knew how hard my boy/girl works every day, they would know that he/she is anything but spoiled.'

A) 'I know that what I am doing will benefit my child.'

B) No response. (Remember that you do not always need to respond to a stranger's unsolicited input.)

B) 'My child has autism.'

Refer to Table 8.1 and remember that this exercise is for your personal benefit. You are not accountable to strangers who interfere in your child-rearing. You also need not respond out of embarrassment. Your child is working hard at developing and is wonderful!

Hurtful remarks are not always intended. As you become more comfortable with your knowledge and with your child and his various behaviors, your confidence will ease any disapproving looks and comments. Confidence can even act to discourage such disapproval altogether.

Table 8.1

Think of your own mental responses and counteracting sentences for various statements you may encounter in the community:

1. **Statement**

    'What are they doing to that child!'

    Responses

    A)_____

    B)_____

2. **Statement**

    'That child is in need of discipline!'

    Responses

    A)_____

    B)_____

3. **Statement**

    'If I were that child's parent, I would…!'

    Responses

    A)_____

    B)_____

4. **Statement**

    _____

    Responses

    A)_____

    B)_____

5. **Statement**

    _____

    Responses

    A)_____

    B)_____

Conclusion

Being an active community member exposes a child to many new learning experiences. With proper preparation and patience, outings can allow children with autism the opportunity to generalize many of the skills that they have already mastered within the home and at school.

In order to promote positive, successful outings, it is important to prepare activities and keep in mind skills that the child can practice actively in the community. These activities can be practiced ahead of time in the home, as well. Alternating between non-preferred activities and activities that the child enjoys will increase the day's overall success. It will also teach the child to tolerate and even enjoy activities that were previously aversive to him.

A variety of reinforcers should be brought along and given to the child periodically throughout the day as a reward for good behavior. Toys and activities from home can be used as substitutes for unsuccessful activities in the community in order to help the child to behave appropriately.

Schedules increase predictability. When schedules are not possible, prepare the child for transitions. Allowing the child to make choices will increase his independence and compliance. Teach him the vocabulary he will need in order to communicate wishes and discomfort.

Finally, remember that every parent has experienced at least one public tantrum. A successful outing is one during which you are confident and comfortable with your incredibly wonderful child, who is learning and growing every day.

Our Story

A Parent's Account

Suzanne Schoenfeld

February second is to me one of those days that is indelibly stamped in one's memory, and no matter how much time passes, it feels like it happened yesterday. On February second, I was to be induced to deliver my second child. On my way out the door to the hospital, I grabbed the mail and took it with me so I would have something to read, as I knew from my past experience that labor and delivery can take quite a while. After checking in and settling myself in my room, I reached for the stack of mail I had brought from home. Bills, bills, bills, junk mail, big manila envelope.

I opened the envelope, not knowing that with this seemingly innocent act my life would be forever altered. Inside were reports concerning my two-and-a-half-years-old son, Jordan. I had been concerned about Jordan's development for quite some time. He seemed like such a bright child, yet there were these little idio-syncracies that made me a little uneasy. For instance, when I called his name, he would never look up from what he was doing, almost as if he were deaf. Yet his ears would prick up at sounds that were almost undetectable to me such as the sound of my husband's footsteps coming down the hall towards our apartment, even before his keys were in the door. He rarely spoke, but he could tap out a rhythm to any song that was playing on the radio. He was the only child I knew who could clap to 'Bingo' without missing a beat.

He was meticulously neat and everything had to be in order. In fact, nothing pleased him more than taking his toys and lining them up in a straight row that would have made a drill sergeant proud. When I would move a toy in the middle of the line-up just a quarter of a centimeter off, he would zoom in on it and immediately put it back in its proper place. He also had an acute sense of smell, so that when we went for walks and we passed a restaurant, I had to run quickly by with him lest he vomit. He was deliriously happy, dancing and reaching for these little bits of dust that only he could see, yet he could never see the big noisy airplanes I pointed out as they flew overhead.

I had to stop taking Jordan with me to the supermarket because he would cry and scream and carry on and try to get out of his stroller as if his very life depended on it. One time a store manager thought I was kidnapping Jordan, because why else would a child carry on that way, and wouldn't let me leave the store until I was able to prove that I was in fact Jordan's mother and not some abductor. If Jordan accidentally went running into a wall, he would just pick himself up and not even cry, but if someone tried to touch him, he would howl as if in pain.

He was also very routine-oriented. For instance, when we handed him a cookie for a snack, he would first put it on the table and then pick it up, and only then would he eat it. Also, if we went to visit friends, we always had to take the same familiar route. If there was traffic and we had to turn down a different street he would cry about it for hours. Even if we had only traveled somewhere only once, he would remember the way. It was truly amazing.

If he went from room to room he would gather up every toy he had and take them with him. Sometimes he would be holding ten to fifteen objects at a time in his little arms. He reminded me of a squirrel hoarding nuts for the duration of the winter.

I guess what bothered me most, though, was the way he ignored me. No matter how much I tried to play with him, he wasn't interested. He preferred to spend his day catching dust particles or banging blocks together for hours. Sometimes he did let me read to him but it was always on his terms. I had voiced my concerns to the pediatrician but it was always the same: 'He's a boy, boys talk later, be patient.' Unsatisfied, I decided to seek an outside opinion as to whether these were just adorable quirks that made Jordan Jordan, or if this was something else entirely.

So there I sat in my hospital bed waiting for my daughter to be born, reading the reports from the outside professionals. It wasn't good news. The reports said that Jordan was difficult to examine, as he wouldn't engage with the examiners, and then continued to list for six pages all of the things he couldn't do. They concluded with the fact that Jordan was currently functioning at the level of a child between the ages of twelve to eighteen months. The recommendation was a preschool program where he could receive speech and occupational therapy, each twice a week for one half-hour session. I knew Jordan had some speech delays but I never imagined it was to this extent. He seemed so bright, always doing little clever things, and no other child in the neighborhood could run as fast as he could. How could it be that this two-and-one-half-years-old was functioning at a level of a one-year-old? And if that was the case, how could the pediatrician not notice such a discrepancy? Especially after I had mentioned my concerns!

I tried to take in all of this information but it was time to push. The mourning would have to wait until after the birth. My daughter was born a little while later, healthy and well, with ten fingers and ten toes. We were very busy those next few days, wrapped up in the joy and responsibility of having a newborn to care for.

Life finally settled into a routine and it was time to focus again on the problem at hand. I enrolled Jordan in a preschool and he received the services that were recommended. I can't say he was very happy to go. He left the house with all of his toys in his hands and pretty much carried them with him throughout the day. When the other children gathered for circle time, he ran over to the other side of the room and stayed by himself as he watched them out of the corner of his eye. At snack time he wouldn't sit near the other children, so they seat-belted him to his chair. He spent a good part of his day sitting in front of a mirror, banging his blocks together.

Jordan remained in this program for a few months with little improvement. Whenever I questioned his teachers regarding his progress they always said, 'He's doing great, really improving,' but I didn't see it. I started demanding more answers but was rebuffed with, 'We don't like to give a label to a child who is so young. Spend more time playing on the floor with him.' After a particularly trying day, I turned to my husband and said, 'Something is not right, there's something they are not telling us.' I took out all of my old psychology textbooks from college and started reading through them to get some sort of clue as to what the problem could be.

I found it on page 633. There was a checklist of behaviors associated with autism, and as I read through the list, I had a terrible sinking feeling in the pit of my stomach that only a parent can know. I could see that Jordan had almost every one of the behaviors mentioned. He lined up his toys, he spun himself around in circles for hours at a time without getting dizzy, he didn't play with children, he viewed people as objects, he did not play with toys unless he was banging two blocks together or spinning the wheels on a car. The list went on and on and I think I checked off almost every one. It was almost as if there was a hidden camera in my house recording every little nuance of Jordan's personality and then transcribing it into this book. I was sure beyond any reasonable doubt that Jordan had autism.

I went to Jordan's school the next day and presented the information I had found to the different team members working with him. They tried to convince me that he was young and that many children have these odd behaviors at his age but they tend to disappear. I would be wasting my time worrying about nothing. I'm not sure I was convinced, because when I went home my husband and I decided to seek out a second opinion. We spent the next few months on a quest for a diagnosis, going from doctor to doctor. We kept getting the same answer. 'He's too young to be diagnosed, let's wait and see what happens when he turns three.' All the doctors said the same thing, so we figured that they must be right. We certainly didn't have as much experience in child development as they did. Still we were uneasy.

Jordan's third birthday came and went and still I didn't see much improvement. I continued taking him to doctors and finally found someone who said he was 'autistic-like' and sent us on our way without any recommendations. In the course of the next few months we received diagnoses of 'autistic-like,' pervasive development disorder (PDD), pervasive development disorder – not otherwise specified (PDD-NOS), and 'autism.' I started doing research on all of these conflicting diagnoses and realized that they were pretty much the same.

The real question was, what were we going to do about it? Most of the doctors just gave a diagnosis without any thought to intervention. The only recommendation we did get was from a doctor who told us to be patient since we were in for a long, terrible haul. He then suggested the same thing as Jordan's school did, which was to play on the floor with Jordan, but he didn't tell us how to even get Jordan on the floor to play with us, let alone look at us!

During my research I came across a book written by a mother who had two children diagnosed with autism and used applied behavior analysis (ABA) to help them. As I read through the book I knew I had found the answer, and that we had to try this intervention with Jordan. I contacted an organization in my town that provides services to children with autism, and spoke to a young girl in charge of behavior training. After I had met with her, and begged her to work privately with Jordan, she finally agreed to set up an ABA program in our home. She, along with two other workers, would work with Jordan after he came home from his preschool.

Excited as I was to start something that I thought could help Jordan, I think I was even more nervous and afraid. Who would these strangers be that would be coming into my house and working with my child? What if the intervention didn't work and he didn't improve? What would we try next?

January seventh was D-Day. It was almost a full year since those initial reports on Jordan and we had lost so much precious time. The doorbell rang, and standing in front of me was a young girl who said she was the therapist. She took Jordan into his room and started working with him immediately. She demanded that he look at her, that he raise his arms over his head, and that he sit quietly in his chair – all without a seat belt! She didn't let him bang his blocks together either. If he wanted to play with them, or with any other toy for that matter, then he had to play with them appropriately. Blocks were for building not banging, cars were for driving not spinning, instruments were for playing, not lining up. Oh, was he angry! No one had ever demanded these things of him before. He struggled against her and her demands but he had nowhere to run to, nowhere to hide. The stranger was on top of his every move and never let him out of her sight for a second! Truth be told, I didn't know what to make of it all myself. I was torn between helping my child break through his autism and protecting him from this stranger who had invaded our lives.

A few weeks passed and things began to settle down. Jordan even began to look forward to his after-school program. The therapist would come and Jordan would push me out of his room so he could be alone to work with her. They worked on all kinds of things together such as how to match, imitate movements, point to items he wanted, and play with toys appropriately. He started looking at us a little more frequently and he learned to sit in a chair beautifully. Little improvements happened every day and soon even friends and family members began to notice them. Three months after the therapist began working with Jordan, I decided to share with the school what we had been doing for Jordan at home. While they all agreed that they had seen improvements in Jordan's all-over relatedness and sitting skills, they were absolutely horrified that we were doing ABA with him. Didn't we know that it was child abuse and we would produce a robotic child? I left that meeting and knew that Jordan would never set foot in that school again. His progress was undeniable. We gradually increased Jordan's hours at home until he received between thirty and forty hours of ABA therapy a week. Having therapists in and out of your house all day long is taxing. Funding a program like this does not come cheap. It wasn't an easy decision financially or emotionally, but it was the right one.

Looking back over the last three years I see a little boy who has come so far. He may not be 'recovered' like the children in the book I had read, but I firmly believe he is where he is today because of ABA. Jordan is currently in a center-based ABA program, learning to read and write like other children his age. We continue to work with him outside the school, using behavioral strategies and applying them to everyday life. He can now pour his own water, dress independently, express his needs and wants, and even say 'I love you.' He still struggles with aspects of speech but he continues to make small gains each day. He is an affectionate son and a loving older brother who loves to play tag with his sister. Some days are better than others, but every day contains some small miracle that we never even thought possible.

References and Resources

Articles

American Psychiatric Association (1994) *Diagnostic and Statistical Manual* (4th edition). Washington, DC: American Psychiatric Association.

Arendt, R. E., MacLean, W. E. Jr., and Baumeister, A. A. (1988) 'Critique of sensory integration therapy and its application in mental retardation.' *American Journal on Mental Retardation 92*, 401–411.

Carr, E. G. and Durand, V. M. (1985) 'Reducing behavior problems through functional communication training.' *Journal of Applied Behavior Analysis 18*, 111–127.

Delmolino, L. M. and Romanczyk, R. G. (1995) 'Facilitated communication: a critical review.' *The Behavior Therapist 18*, 2, 27–30.

Lovaas, O. I. and Smith, T. (1989) 'A comprehensive behavioral theory of autistic children: paradigm for research and treatment.' *Journal of Behavior Therapy and Experimental Psychiatry 20*, 17–29.

Rimland, B. and Edelson, S. M. (1994) 'The effects of auditory integration training on autism.' *American Journal of Speech–Language Pathology 3*, 16–24.

Rincover, A. (1978) 'Sensory extinction: a procedure for elimination of self-stimulatory behavior in psychotic children.' *Journal of Abnormal Child Psychology 6*, 299–301.

Rutter, M. and Schopler, E. (eds) (1978) *Autism: A Reprisal of Concepts and Treatment* pp.1–25. London and New York: Plenum Press.

Schopler, E. and Olley, J. G. (1982) 'Comprehensive educational services for autistic children: the TEACCH model.' In C. R. Reynolds and T. B. Gutkin (eds) *Handbook of School Psychology* (pp. 626–643). New York: Wiley.

Books

Attwood, T. (1998) *Asperger's Syndrome: A Guide for Parents and Professionals.* London: Jessica Kingsley Publishers.

Baker, B.L., Brightman, A.J., Blacher, J.B., Heifetz, L.J. and Hinshaw, S.P. (1997) *Steps to Independence: Teaching Everyday Skills to Children with Special Needs* (3rd edition). Baltimore, MD: Brookes Publishing.

Beyer, J. and Gammeltoft, L. (1999) *Autism and Play.* London: Jessica Kingsley Publishers.

Briggs, F. (1995) *Developing Personal Safety Skills in Children with Disabilities.* London: Jessica Kingsley Publishers.

Carr, E.G., Levin, L. *et al.* (1994) *Communication-Based Intervention for Problem Behavior.* Baltimore, MD: Brookes Publishing Co.

Durand, V.M. (1998) *Sleep Better! A Guide to Improving Sleep for Children with Special Needs.* Baltimore, MD: Brookes Publishing Co.

Durand, V.M. (1990) *Severe Behavior Problems.* New York NY: Guildford Press.

Fling, E.R. (2000) *Eating an Artichoke: A Mother's Perspective on Asperger Syndrome.* London: Jessica Kingsley Publishers.

Foxx, R. (1982) *Increasing Behaviors of Persons with Severe Retardation and Autism.* Champaign IL: Research Press.

Foxx, R. (1982) *Decreasing Behaviors of Severely Retarded and Autistic Persons.* Champaign IL: Research Press.

Freeman, S. and Dake, L. (1996) *Teach Me Language: A Language Manual for Children with Autism, Aspergers Syndrome and Related Disorders.* Langley BC: SKF Books.

Gray, C. (1994) *Social Stories ... All New Stories: Teaching Social Skills.* Arlington TX: Future Horizons Inc.

Gray, C. (1994) *Comic Strip Conversations.* Arlington TX: Future Horizons Inc.

Gray, C. (1993) *The Original Social Story Book.* Arlington TX: Future Horizons Inc.

Harris, S.L. (1994) *Siblings of Children with Autism: Guide for Families.* Bethesda MD: Woodbine House.

Harris, S.L. and Handleman, J.S. (1994) *Preschool and Education Programs for Children with Autism.* Austin TX: Pro-Ed.

Harris, S.L. and Weiss, M.J. (1998) *Right from the Start: Behavioral Intervention for Young Children with Autism.* Bethesda MD: Woodbine House.

Hileman, C. (1997) *Point, Click and Learn.* Arlington TX: Future Horizons Inc.

Keenan, M., Kerr, K.P. and Dillenburger, K. (1999) *Parents' Education as Autism Therapists: Applied Behavior Analysis in Context.* London: Jessica Kingsley Publishers.

Koegel, L.K., Koegel, R.L. and Dunlap, G. (1996) *Positive Behavioral Support: Including People with Difficult Behavior in the Community.* Baltimore MD: Paul H. Brookes Publishing Co.

Koegel, R. and Koegel, L.K. (1995) *Teaching Children with Autism.* Baltimore MD: Paul H. Brookes Publishing Co.

Lovaas, O.I. (1991) *Teaching Developmentally Disabled Children: The Me Book.* Austin TX: Pro-ed.

Lowman, D.K. and Murphy, S.M. (1998) *The Educator's Guide to Feeding Children with Disabilities.* Baltimore MD: Paul H. Brookes Publishing Co.

Luiselli, J.K. and Cameron, M.J. (1998) *Antecedent Control: Innovative Approaches to Behavioral Support.* Baltimore MD: Paul H. Brookes Publishing Co.

Martin, G. and Pear, J. (1992) *Behavior Modification: What it is and How to Do it.* Englewood Cliffs NJ: Simon and Schuster Company.

Maurice, C. (1994) *Let Me Hear Your Voice.* New York NY: Random House, Inc.

Maurice, C., Green, G. and Luce, S.C. (1996) *Behavioral Intervention for Young Children with Autism: A Manual for Parents and Professionals.* Austin TX: Pro-ed.

McClannahan, L.E. and Krantz, P.J. (1999) *Activity Schedules for Children with Autism: Teaching Independent Behavior.* Bethesda MD: Woodbine House.

Meyer, D.J. (1997) *Views from Our Shoes: Growing Up with a Brother or Sister with Special Needs.* Bethesda MD: Woodbine House.

Newman, S. (1999) *Small Steps Forward.* London: Jessica Kingsley Publishers.

Powers, M.D. (2000) *Children with Autism: A Parent's Guide* (2nd edition). Bethesda MD: Woodbine House.

Romanczyk, R.G., Lockshin, S., and Matey, L. (1994) *The Individualized Goal Selection Curriculum (IGS)*. New York NY: Appalachian.

Schwartz, S. and Heller Miller, J.E. (1996) *The New Language of Toys: Teaching Communication Skills to Children with Special Needs.* Bethesda MD: Woodbine House.

Siegel, B. (1996) *The World of the Autistic Child: Understanding and Treating Autistic Spectrum Disorders.* New York NY: Oxford University Press, Inc.

Siegel, B. and Silverstein, S.C. (1994) *What About Me? Growing Up with a Developmentally Disabled Sibling.* New York NY: Plenum.

Staub, D. (1998) *Delicate Threads: Friendships Between Children with and without Special Needs in Inclusive Settings.* Bethesda MD: Woodbine House.

Thompson, M. (1996) *Andy and his Yellow Frisbee.* Bethesda MD: Woodbine House.

Wheeler, M. (1999) *Toilet Training for Individuals with Autism and Related Disorders: A Comprehensive Guide for Parents and Teachers.* Arlington TX: Future Horizons Inc.

Videos

Autism Perspectives
Autism Insights
Making Contact – Sensory Integration and Autism
Media/Publication Division Continuing Education Programs of America
PO Box 52
Peoria, IL 61650
(309) 263-0310

Autism: 'What Can Parents Do?'
California School of Professional Psychology, LA

Baby's First Impressions Series

Seasons
Sounds
Head to Toe
Food Fun

Numbers
Letters
Available through Different Roads to Learning (see catalogs below)

Behavior Modification Training
Community Services for Autistic Adults and Children
751 Twinbrook Parkway
Rockville, MD
301-762-1650

Behavioral Treatment of Autistic Children
Focus International, Inc.
14 Oregon Drive
Huntington Station, NY 11746
(516) 549-5320
(800) 843-0305

Bridges for Children with Autism Series
Bridges
PO Box 35
Burnt Hills, NY 12027
(888) 222-8273

Brothers and Sisters: A Video About Siblings for Siblings of Children with Disabilities
Autism Society of British Columbia

Discrete Trial Teaching
New York Families for Autistic Children
83-10 149th Avenue
Queens, NY 11414
(718) 641-6711
Fax: (718) 843-0036

Managing Behaviors in Community Settings
Indiana Resource Center for Autism
Indiana Institute on Disability and Community
2853 E. Tenth Street
Bloomington, IN 47408-2696
(812) 855-6508
Fax: (812) 855-9630

Special Kids Videos
Body Parts and Grooming
Animals, Birds and Fish
Things in a Day
Getting Ready
Spelling
A Day at School
Lets Go To…

Special Kids
PO Box 462
Muskego, WI 53150
1-800-Kids-153
Fax: (262) 679-5992
www.specialkids1.com

Teaching People with Developmental Disabilities
Research Press
Department 141
PO Box 9177
Champaign, IL 61826
(217) 352-3273

The Age of Autism
Mark-It Television (in association with the National Autistic Society)
7 Quarry Way
Stapleton, Bristol BS16 1UP
United Kingdom
(0117) 939-1117
Fax: (0117) 939-1118

What Do We Do Next?
Families for Early Autism Treatment
6220 West Peregrine Way
Tucson, AZ 85745
(520) 743-1223

For a variety of additional autism and child development videos, contact:
Child Development Media Inc.
5632 Van Nuys Blvd., Suite 286
Van Nuys, CA 91401
(800) 405-8942
Fax: (818) 994-0153
www.childdevmedia.com

Catalogs

ABC School Supply
3312 N. Berkeley Lake Road
Duluth, GA 30096-9419
(800) 669-4222
http://www.abcschoolsupply.com

Autism and Developmental Disabilities Resource Catalog
Family Resource Services, Inc.
231 Columbia Road 61
PO Box 1146
Magnolia, AR 71754
1-800-501-0139

Different Roads to Learning, LLC
12 West 18th Street, Suite 3 East
New York, NY 10011
(800) 853-1057
http://www.difflearn.com

Kaplan
P.O. Box 609
1310 Lewisville-Clemmons Road
Lewisville, NC 27023-0609
(800) 334-2014
www.kaplanco.com

Lakeshore Learning Materials
2695 E. Dominguez Street
P.O. Box 6261
Carson, CA 90749
(800) 421-5354
www.lakeshorelearning.com

Super Duper Publications
Speech and Language Materials
Dept. SDM99
P.O. Box 24997
Greenville, SC 29616-2497
(800) 277-8737
www.superduperinc.com

Super Duper School Company
Department A
P.O. Box 24997
Greenville, SC 29616-2497
(800) 227-8737

Organizations

Autism Research Institute
4182 Adams Avenue
San Diego, CA, 92116
(619) 563-6840

Autism Society of America Inc.
7910 Woodmont Avenue Suite 650
Bethesda, MD, 20814-3015
(301) 657-0881

Autism Society of Canada
129 Yorkville Avenue Suite 202
Toronto, Ontario M5R 1C4 Canada
(416) 922-0302

Autism Treatment Services of Canada
404-94th Ave SE
Calgary, AB
T2J 0E8
(403) 253-6961

COSAC (Center for Outreach Services for the Autism Community)
1450 Parkside Avenue Suite 22
Ewing, NJ, 08638
(609) 883-5509

The National Autistic Society
393 City Road
London EC1V 1NE UK
(020) 7833 2299

Pro-Ed (publishing company)
8700 Shoal Creek Boulevard
Austin, TX, 78758-6897
(512) 4513246

Project TEACCH
UNC, Chapel Hill
Chapel Hill, NC, 27599

Sibling Information Network
Department of Educational Psychology
Box U-64 The University of Connecticut
Storrs, CT, 06268
(203) 486-4034

The Association for Science in Autism Treatment
575 Coal Valley Road, Suite 109
Pittsburgh, PA 15025
jcdavin@autism-treatment.org

Websites

www.ani.ac
www.aspergers.com
www.autism.com
www.autism.com/ari
www.autism.org
www.autism-info.com
www.autism-pdd.net/autism.htm
www.autism-resources.com
www.autism-society.org
www.autism-spectrum.com
www.autism-uk.ed.ac.uk
www.csaac.org
www.educationplanet.com/search/Education/Special-Education/Autism
www.familyvillage.wisc.edu/index.htmlx
www.feat.org

www.kidsource.com/nichcy/autism.html
www.ncld.org
www.mugsy.org
www.nichcy.org
www.parentbookstore.com/autism.htm
www.paulbunyan.net/users/cbsolson/BOlson1/autism/links.html
www.pecs.com
www.playsteps.com
www.seattlechildrens.org/sibsupp
www.suite101.com/links.cfm/autism
www.support-group.com
http://thoth.stetson.edu/ShapesForLearning
www.toytips.com

For further help, contact your state offices:
Director of Special Education
Protection and Advocacy
Vocational Rehabilitation Agency
Parent Training and Information Projects

Index